SEVEN WORDS

Seven Words
Listening to Christ from the Cross

Seven Words
978-1-7910-0781-2
978-1-7910-0782-9 eBook

Seven Words: DVD
978-1-7910-0785-0

Seven Words: Leader Guide
978-1-7910-0783-6
978-1-7910-0784-3 eBook

Also by Susan Robb

Called: Hearing and Responding to God's Voice

SEVEN WORDS

LISTENING TO CHRIST
FROM THE CROSS

Susan Robb

Abingdon Press / Nashville

SEVEN WORDS
Listening to Christ from the Cross

Library of Congress Control Number: 2020946777
ISBN-13: 978-1-7910-0781-2

20 21 22 23 24 25 26 27 28 29 — 10 9 8 7 6 5 4 3 2 1
MANUFACTURED IN THE UNITED STATES OF AMERICA

In memory of my parents,
John and Floy,
and also my brother, Mike,
and dear cousin, Brenda,
whose last words at the end of each day,
and life, were the ones that were
most important to hear: "I love you."

Contents

INTRODUCTION

As a minister, I've had the holy privilege of experiencing the intimacy of being at the bedside of those who were near death or in the hospital with those going into surgery not knowing what the outcome might be. Almost always the messages of the dying, or of those who think the chances of death are high, are poignant.

"We've had a good life together."

"Everything is going to be okay."

"I want you to take care of each other."

"You'll never know how proud I am to have been your father (or mother, grandparent, son, or daughter)."

Whether they are reassuring, poignant, or offer instructions for the future, the last words of anyone who is near death, or thinks that life may be coming to an end, almost always communicate in some form or fashion, "I love you more than you can know." On their deathbeds, people tend to convey messages that are most important to them; words that they most want their families and friends to hear. What I've also discovered is that family members always want to lean in and listen to these last words because they are eager to hear what the one they love most has to say—a message that they will always remember, a message that might be just for them.

Jesus's last words, uttered as he was dying on Good Friday, offer us the opportunity to lean in and listen closely for messages that are for us. These statements, collected from the various Gospel accounts, have traditionally been called the seven last words of Jesus. It is particularly important to listen to them during Lent, because Jesus calls on us to go on the same journey that led him to Golgotha. According to the Gospel writers, he made that call graphically, painfully explicit: "If any want to become my followers, let them...take up their cross and follow me" (Mark 8:34). To hear Jesus's dying words as guideposts for our own journey is to reclaim the power of the words to two beautiful hymns: "Must Jesus bear the cross alone, / and all the world go free? / No, there's a cross for everyone, / and there's a cross for me."[1] Christ's words become, for us, not merely dying words but words that show us how to live. They point the way as we seek to carry out the mission that we undertake when we commit to follow him and "Lift high the cross, the love of Christ proclaim / till all the world adore his sacred name."[2]

Though Jesus's dying words from the cross are few, they reflect the same tenderness, the same compassion, the same forgiveness, the same unconditional love, the same giving of himself, the same faith and trust, and the same desire to welcome everyone into his kingdom as his actions exhibited in life. In the midst of unimaginable cruelty and taunting, Jesus offers forgiveness to his persecutors, and his killers. In the midst of suffering, he offers a human cry that, when followed to its scriptural conclusion, leads to reassurance, hope, life, and joy for all humanity. As he looks upon his mother for the last time, he calls his followers into a new community, a different way of understanding family. And in his final breath as a human, he trustingly gives himself back to the One who breathed life into the first human beings.

When we look at Jesus's last words in each of the Gospels, it may be surprising to learn that not all of them are recorded in all four accounts. In fact, only one of these sayings is quoted in more than one Gospel, and six of the seven last words are unique either to John—the only Gospel whose author is presented as an eyewitness to the crucifixion—or to Luke. Here is a quick breakdown:

Matthew and Mark:
> "My God, my God, why have you forsaken me?"
> (Matthew 27:46; Mark 15:34)

Luke:
> "Father, forgive them; for they do not know what they are doing." (23:34)

> "Truly I tell you, today you will be with me in Paradise." (23:43)

> "Father, into your hands I commend my spirit." (23:46)

John:
> "'Woman, here is your son.'... 'Here is your mother.'"
> (19:26-27)

> "I am thirsty." (19:28)

> "It is finished." (19:30)

One might wonder why each Gospel writer included such differing last words. Why wouldn't each writer record all of Jesus's statements? I believe that these statements are not contradictory, but that each author chose to represent Jesus's particular message(s) for the benefit of his particular community. In addition, each of those authors would have had access to reports of various witnesses to Jesus's crucifixion. Those witnesses would not have included all of the same information or details, just as witnesses to a crime or an earthshaking event will report details that made the biggest impression on them.

We see this pattern throughout the Gospels, not just in the accounts of Jesus's death that emphasize varying details. For example, some of the most familiar Bible stories we may have learned as children, such as the parable of the good Samaritan and the story of the prodigal son and loving father, are recorded only by Luke. Some of Jesus's other parables, like the parable of the wheat and weeds, can be found only in Matthew. Only Luke tells of the angel's visitation to Mary, and only John tells us the story of Jesus and his detailed conversations with the Samaritan woman at the well and Mary Magdalene at the garden tomb.

Briefly now, let's look at each of Jesus's seven "last words." We'll explore them much more deeply in the chapters that follow. For now, let's stop long enough only to consider how these particular memories of what Jesus said from the cross, taken together, give us a more complete picture of who he is and what he calls us to do. Consider, too, how each of these dying words might have been the special words that each Gospel writer believed that his audience needed to hear.

Matthew and Mark report what is known as Jesus's cry of dereliction, "My God, my God, why have you forsaken me?" While these words appear to express desperation and lost hope, if we look at the context from which Jesus draws them (Psalm 22) and follow them through to their scriptural conclusion, we discover not a cry of abandonment but one of trust, reassurance, and hope. As a people who also sometimes feel as if God's presence and care are missing in our lives, we need to explore the hope Jesus wishes for us to experience in our own moments of deep darkness.

Not only do Luke's three messages emphasize the complete intimacy and trust Jesus has in his "Father" in heaven, but they also reverberate with Jesus's deepest desires for all of humanity. For any of us who have ever sought forgiveness, worried that we were too far gone to receive God's mercy and grace, or struggled mightily to take up the cross of forgiving those who have hurt us the most, lean in and listen. Jesus offers in death, as in life, loving reassurance and a radically counterintuitive path toward inner peace and living into the paradise of God's kingdom—forever but also (and especially) in the here and now.

Matthew, Mark, and Luke are known as the Synoptic (from Greek words that mean to "see together") Gospels because they tell the story of Jesus's life and death through the same "eye" or lens. While details and facts are paramount in the Synoptic Gospels, the Gospel of John is much different. In the Fourth Gospel, symbolism reigns. Each of Jesus's words in John has not only a literal meaning but a deeper, symbolic one as well. While Jesus literally leaves his mother in the care of his dear friend out of concern for her, he also defines a new family of faith that reaches far beyond the old bonds of kin, tribe, and nation. While he shares in our humanity as he experiences physical thirst on the cross, on a symbolic level the one who offers "living water" to all who believe in him is poured out for the world. On a literal level, he drinks sour wine that the soldiers give him; on a symbolic level, he drinks from the cup of suffering that, at the time of his arrest, he tells Peter that the Father has given him. On one level, he announces that his earthly life has ended; on a spiritual level, he declares that he has finished the work on earth that the Father gave him to do. Jesus's messages to us in John's Gospel are multifaceted. At times, they might even seem contradictory to us. If you've ever wondered about your place and purpose in this family of faith called Christianity; if you've ever been spiritually bone-dry and thirsty for more in your life or thirsty for more for the world; if you've ever wondered what work Jesus and the Father call you to on earth, Jesus's words to you from the cross in the Gospel of John will bring you a mixture of comfort, inspiration, challenge, and cross-carrying.

Since we cannot know for certain the order in which Jesus spoke these words from the cross, I will follow a traditional ordering of them (we'll also study two of the sayings in one chapter to allow the book study to be utilized during the six weeks corresponding to Lent):

1. "Father, forgive them; for they do not know what they are doing."
2. "Today you will be with me in Paradise."
3. "My God, my God, why have you forsaken me?"
4. "'Woman, here is your son.'. . . 'Here is your mother.'"
5. "I am thirsty."
6. "Into your hands I commend my spirit" and "It is finished."

For many of us, spending six weeks at the cross—a place of suffering, sorrow, and shame—may seem daunting. I admit that, at one time in my life, I preferred to go straight from waving palm branches in celebration of Jesus's triumphal entry into Jerusalem on Palm Sunday to singing the glory of his resurrection on Easter morning. Spending too much time dwelling on the last moments of Jesus's life, sitting in the dark of Good Friday, reading or hearing of the brutality of the cross—all were things I would rather have avoided. I much preferred moving from joy to joy.

Over the years, however, I've come to understand and cherish the importance of engaging in the entire season of Lent and Easter. While many of us naturally wish to avoid the painful reality of the cross, it is from there that Jesus speaks and shows his deepest love for us. It is from the cross that Jesus's full humanity draws us closest to him. It is from the cross, as Jesus breathes his last breath and speaks his last words, that his deep trust in the Father and his divine glory are revealed. And it is in the example of the cross that Jesus calls us into a life where we find God's kingdom through love that is willing to give freely of itself to others.

The reality is that preparing for the joy of Easter by walking with Jesus through his last days, and taking time to stand by him and listen to his words from the cross, offers a depth of understanding and spiritual power that one simply cannot experience by moving only from joy to joy. It is the difference between eating only dessert from meal to meal compared to consuming multiple courses of an expertly prepared gourmet dinner. The first may leave you with a bit of a sugar high, but it can also leave you malnourished. The second not only is nourishing but also leaves your soul deeply satisfied.

To skip the cross and focus only on Easter is like wanting to bypass all of the months of training and sacrifice it takes to prepare for a marathon and go straight to the elation of crossing the finish line. Without training and conditioning, we won't make it. Just as the training is a necessary part of the journey by which we are able to reach the end of the race, the cross is part of our journey, individually and as a community, to Easter. It is part of our journey toward being able to say, when we reach our end, "It is finished. I have completed the mission you gave me," or as the apostle Paul would say, "I have finished the race, I have kept the faith. From now on there is reserved for me the crown of righteousness, which the Lord...will give me on that day" (2 Timothy 4:7-8).

And so I invite you to join me on this Lenten journey, which we follow by way of the cross, and to listen closely to what could be some of the most meaningful and powerful words we will ever hear.

CHAPTER 1

Father,
Forgive
Them

Chapter 1

FATHER, FORGIVE THEM

Two others also, who were criminals, were led away to be put to death with him. When they came to the place that is called The Skull, they crucified Jesus there with the criminals, one on his right and one on his left. Then Jesus said, "Father, forgive them; for they do not know what they are doing." And they cast lots to divide his clothing.

Luke 23:32-34

The week of Passover had begun with such promise for Jesus's followers, who joined the many pilgrims who had gathered in Jerusalem to celebrate the great feast commemorating God's deliverance of the Jews from slavery in Egypt. On Sunday, crowds lined the streets of Jerusalem as Jesus, mounted on a donkey, made a triumphal entry into the city. For those who knew the Jewish scriptures, this was a much hoped for and welcomed sign. Through this single prophetic action—riding a donkey from the Mount of Olives into Jerusalem—Jesus announced he was the expected Messiah, come to save Israel, fulfilling the words of the prophet (Zechariah 9:9). Every devout Jew who saw him would have known what Jesus's prophetic action meant. Excitement swelled, as did the crowd, as the city buzzed with the news of Jesus's presence. Joyful followers paved the road Jesus traveled with their cloaks as they shouted, "Blessed is the king / who comes in the name of the Lord!" (Luke 19:38). Others waved palm branches and joined the chorus with, "Hosanna to the Son of David!" (Matthew 21:9). At least some among the crowd hoped for a military king, a new David, to deliver the people from their enemies (in this case, the hated Roman occupiers). Jesus is a king, all right, but not the kind that so many hoped for.

By Thursday evening things had gone horribly wrong. Before the sun rose on Friday, Jesus was betrayed by his friend and disciple, Judas, and arrested by the temple police, who mocked and beat him. To add insult to injury, Jesus's most ardent disciple, Peter, publicly denied that he even knew him. The chief priests—who disagreed with Jesus's interpretation of the law, feared that the Romans would see him as a dangerous threat, and had been seeking an opportunity to kill him—declared Jesus guilty of blasphemy. They took Jesus to the Roman governor of Judea, Pontius Pilate, on trumped up charges of political subversion, of inciting tax evasion, and of saying that he is a king. These charges, if true, were obvious challenges to Roman authority. While Rome appointed local puppet rulers like Herod, there was only one emperor. Not paying taxes was paramount to sedition. If the Jewish religious authorities could convince Pilate that Jesus was trying to mount a political rebellion—there had been plenty of others before—Rome would treat Jesus as it had so many other rabble-rousers: death by crucifixion. Some of the religious leaders, convinced that no one worth following could come from a backwater like Nazareth, saw Jesus as a usurper and blasphemer. Others, more conflicted about his identity, saw his signs and miracles as evidence he had been sent by God but also worried that, if Jesus were allowed to continue, the Romans would destroy them all. The crowds that cheered Jesus's entry into the city played right in the fears of Pilate and Herod—and worked in the religious authorities' favor.

After individually interrogating Jesus, neither Pilate nor Herod the puppet king deemed him guilty of any offense meriting crucifixion. The Roman governor, though concerned about the claim that Jesus was a king, nevertheless told the assembled crowd that he found no fault with Jesus. But in what might have seemed to Jesus like an especially cruel turn of events, the crowd that had been so enthusiastic days earlier now shouted, with some goading by their religious leaders, for the release of the criminal Barabbas—and for the one they had hailed as the Son of David to be crucified. Perhaps they were disappointed and outraged that he didn't produce an army to defeat Rome. Perhaps they were easily swayed. Maybe it wasn't even the same crowd that lined the road for Jesus when he entered the city. We can't know for certain. What we do know is that Pilate became fearful when the religious leaders told him, "If you release this man, you are no friend of the emperor. Everyone who claims to be a king sets himself against the emperor" (John 19:12). In the end, Pilate capitulated, literally washing his hands of the whole affair.

Luke spares us the gory details, but Jesus is treated as other criminals slated for execution by crucifixion. He is beaten and flogged, spat upon and ridiculed, stripped of his clothing, and led away to the place of his execution, a hill appropriately named The Skull for the features of its rock formations. There he is crucified with two criminals, one on his right and one on his left. Luke devotes as much space to what Jesus has to say from the cross as he does to the other details of the crucifixion. It's not a coincidence. He wants us, as readers receiving the gospel message from him, to lean in and listen, starting with a jaw-dropping statement about radical forgiveness.

FATHER, FORGIVE THEM:
BUT WHO ARE *THEY*?

From the cross, the instrument of his execution and pain, Jesus speaks words that reflect the depth of God's love and desire for all of humanity. He lives out the words in death that he taught in his Sermon on the Plain:

> *"Love your enemies, do good to those who hate you,...*
> *pray for those who abuse you....*
>
> *"If you love those who love you, what credit is that to*
> *you? For even sinners love those who love them....But*
> *love your enemies, do good....Your reward will be*
> *great, and you will be children of the Most High; for he*
> *is kind to the ungrateful and the wicked. Be merciful,*
> *just as your Father is merciful."*
>
> Luke 6:27-28, 32, 35-36

Having endured the humiliation of betrayal, cruel beatings and mockery from the soldiers, and the prolonged torture and agony of crucifixion, Jesus, in the depth of his pain, doesn't curse those who have mistreated him, as many who were crucified did. Instead, he begins to pray, "Father, forgive them; for they do not know what they are doing" (Luke 23:34).

His prayer raises one obvious question: "Who are *they*?" The soldiers who nailed Jesus to a cross—and who were just doing their job? The crowd who, for whatever reason, was given a choice and yet demanded Jesus's execution? Herod, who treated Jesus with nothing but contempt? Pilate, who, with crumbling convictions, refused to stand firm against the swelling tide of the crowd's desires? The religious leaders, who surely would have been horrified had they understood their responsibility in killing the long-awaited Messiah? Judas, the betrayer? Peter, the denier? Yes. The answer is "all of the above."

But it is also us.

We help crucify Jesus when we get caught up in crowd mentality and say or condone things that go against what we profess to believe and are called to practice as Jesus's followers—things we would never say or condone if we were standing alone. We assist in crucifying Jesus when, like Pilate, we fail to stand up for what we know is right and rationalize to ourselves the doing of wrong. We crucify Jesus little by little when we fail to have regard for how our words and deeds harm others, putting our own interests above theirs, and when we don't grasp the depth of the ways in which we break the hearts of those we love.

If we're honest with ourselves, we need to recognize our own everyday betrayals of Jesus. He has already prepared us for that level of self-reflection by reminding us that the way we treat (or fail to treat) "the least of these" among us is how we have treated him (Matthew 25:40). He calls us to see the divine image of God in everyone we meet. So when I injure someone's spirit with a backhanded comment, I have been brutal not only to that person but also to Jesus. When a lonely or hospitalized or incarcerated person goes unvisited, or a word goes unkept, I, like Peter, have denied Jesus. When I am carried along on the tide of popular vitriolic opinion or I don't raise my voice for the innocent or the disenfranchised, I become the crowd that yelled, "Crucify him!"

So what is Jesus saying to me, as one of his crucifiers? What does he want me to hear?

AMAZING, INCONCEIVABLE, UNIMAGINABLE GRACE

It is beyond the scope of our imagination that, in the midst of being treated with such contempt, violence, and cruelty, the one being tortured would offer a prayer of grace for his tormentors. Try wrapping your head around that. Jesus does not wait until after the triumph of his resurrection to think about forgiveness. He does not wait for those who had a hand in his betrayal, torture, and death to repent. He asks the Father to forgive his killers even as he is being killed. He injects forgiveness into the worst act that any human being could possibly have committed—the murder of God's own Son.

Not only that: Jesus offers his crucifiers an excuse. He intercedes on their behalf with the Father. Don't hold this against them, he says. They do not realize what they are doing. They do not understand the dimensions of this act.

In the process, Jesus leaves open the door to repentance. He says that his killers—all of them, all of us—should not be forever defined by the worst thing they ever did. When we understand that, then we begin to grasp the power of the gospel.

Remember the story that Luke tells of the woman who crashes the dinner party that Simon the Pharisee is hosting for Jesus (Luke 7:36-50)? We never even learn her name—only that she is notorious in the city as a sinner. Luke never records any words she may have spoken in her encounter with Jesus as she kissed his feet, washed them with her tears, dried them with her hair, and then anointed them with ointment. What matters is that she somehow understood the power of what Jesus offered—the power to forgive sins, the power to set her free from the burden of shame and guilt and judgment. In the end, Simon comprehended Jesus's lesson: those for whom an impossible debt has been canceled will have a greater appreciation of the power of forgiveness than someone whose debt is smaller.

John Newton, the English ship captain who carried kidnapped Africans into slavery, experienced that power too. Though he shared responsibility for the bondage, suffering, and deaths of fellow human beings, those sins did not ultimately define who he was in God's eyes. "Forgive him, Father," Jesus might have said of Newton. "He did not truly understand the magnitude of what he was doing to your children." Newton expressed the unfathomable power of forgiveness in words we know by heart: "Amazing grace! How sweet the sound that saved a wretch like me!"[1] And you.

FINDING FORGIVENESS: LEARNING TO SAY 'I'M SORRY'

Love Story, a movie tearjerker from many years ago, was marketed with a tagline that became well known: "Love means never having to say you're sorry."[2] While this may sound romantic, it's also completely absurd. If we want to find relief from guilt and shame for what we have done and for what we have left undone; if we want to have meaningful, loving relationships with our spouses, families, friends, and colleagues, we need to learn to say, "I'm sorry. Will you forgive me?" That is why my husband and I, when we teach a class for engaged and newly married couples, begin one session by saying, "Some of the most important words you will ever say to each other in your marriage, after 'I love you,' will be 'I'm sorry.' We realize that these words may not be common in some of your vocabularies right now, so right now, just for practice, turn to your partner and say 'I'm sorry.'" The couples always smile at each other, say "I'm sorry," and then chuckle a little nervously. Then we say, "See, that wasn't so hard! For your homework this week, we want you to find a moment when you've done something worthy of these words and practice them. We bet you'll find more than one opportunity!"

Learning to say "I'm sorry" is important not only for fostering and healing relationships with friends and family but also for fostering a deep spiritual life as well. When our words or actions bring harm to another person, it's important to acknowledge them and ask for forgiveness. Just as important is adjusting our actions so that those harmful behaviors aren't repeated. The biblical term for this is "repentance." To repent literally means to "turn around" or "go a different direction." It means turning from harmful behaviors to ones that are loving. It's what the prodigal son does, literally and figuratively, when in the depth of his misery he decides to turn around and go home to his father (Luke 15:17-19). Biblically, it means turning back toward God and the behaviors that reflect the kingdom of God on earth as it is in heaven. John the Baptist called this bearing "fruits worthy of repentance" (3:8).

Sometimes people will come to me burdened with guilt or shame. They have sought forgiveness from those they've hurt and from God. They've turned their lives around, and yet they worry about their forgiveness. They worry they haven't done enough to make up for the harm and hurt they have inflicted on others. How can they be assured of God's forgiveness? Do you ever feel that way? I have. John Wesley, the founder of Methodism, did too.

As I write this paragraph, it is the anniversary of Aldersgate Day, the day John Wesley, who was already a devout priest in the Church of England, attended a prayer service at a church on Aldersgate Street in London in 1738. Wesley had struggled with assurance of God's love and forgiveness. It was in that service, as someone read from Martin Luther's *Preface to the Epistle to the Romans*, that he felt his heart "strangely warmed." In his journal, he described his experience in this way: "I felt I did trust in Christ, Christ alone, for salvation; and an assurance was given me that He had taken away my sins, even mine, and saved me from the law of sin and death."[3] Wesley realized that his salvation, his forgiveness, and the outpouring of God's love for him were not about how much more he could do for God, but about what God had already done for him through Jesus Christ.

Fortunately, we don't have to go searching for forgiveness as if it were some hidden treasure. We know where to find it. The prodigal son knew to set a course for home, where his loving father had been waiting patiently for him all along and saw him while he was still a long way off. We find our forgiveness at the foot of the cross, where Jesus experienced our humanity at its worst, offered his life, and spoke the world-changing words, "Father, forgive them." The question is not whether we can find forgiveness. The question is whether we will accept it—and, in the process, accept God's invitation into a life marked by love, mercy, and grace.

There is part of a communion liturgy based on Paul's Letter to the Romans (see Romans 5:8) that I especially love. In my congregation, after we recite a prayer of confession—a public "I'm sorry" to God— the minister (or celebrant) declares, "Christ died for us while we were yet sinners. That proves God's love for us. In the name of Jesus Christ, you are forgiven." When I am the celebrant, my favorite part of that liturgy follows as the congregation responds by saying to me, "In the name of Jesus Christ *you* are forgiven. Glory to God. Amen."

May you, as a fellow crucifier of Jesus, experience in the core of your being the awe-inspiring power of forgiveness that Christ offered you 2,000 years ago. That same assurance is available to you today and every day.

IMITATING JESUS

Some have wondered why Jesus would have prayed, "Father, forgive them," when elsewhere in the Gospel of Luke, Jesus directly forgives people's sins. Jesus says to the paralyzed man who is brought to him for healing, "Friend, your sins are forgiven you" (Luke 5:20). He says of the sinful woman who crashed the dinner party, "'Her sins, which were many, have been forgiven; hence she has shown great love.'... Then he said to her, 'Your sins are forgiven'" (7:47-48).

So why didn't Jesus just say, "I forgive you, because you don't know what you are doing"? One reason is that Jesus's actions were meant to fulfill scripture. The prophet Isaiah says of the suffering servant, "He bore the sin of many, / and made intercession for the transgressors" (Isaiah 53:12). And this is the hard part. It may be that Jesus prays to the Father to set an example for followers who suffer innocently and unjustly.

The thought that Jesus asks God to forgive his killers has caused a great deal of controversy surrounding this prayer/verse, which does not appear in many early manuscripts although it's in a number of others. Why the discrepancy? Among the various theories, some argue that the verse was added by a scribe who may have had knowledge of Jesus's prayer that Luke did not possess. Or it may have been added by those who thought that if the Jewish authorities had realized that Jesus was the Son of God, they never would have crucified him. Yet another theory, which I believe makes sense, is that the verse may have been removed from some manuscripts by Christian copyists in the second century as tensions increased between Christians and Jews. They may have found the verse morally reprehensible because Christians were still being relentlessly persecuted and martyred.[4] I lean toward the theory of omission because Jesus's prayer of forgiveness complements Jesus's teachings earlier in Luke's Gospel, and because Jesus's example was imitated by the first known Christian martyr. As Stephen is being stoned for sharing the good news of Jesus he cries out, "Lord, do not hold this sin against them" (Acts 7:60).

Jesus's words are meant for us to hear and imitate. Matthew's Gospel records that Peter asks Jesus, "Lord, if another member of the church sins against me, how often should I forgive? As many as seven times?" (Matthew 18:21).

Jesus answers: "Not seven times, but, I tell you, seventy-seven times" (18:22). In other words, forgiveness is beyond counting, and for disciples it is not optional.

To make his point unmistakably clear, Jesus tells a parable about two servants. One servant owes the king 10,000 silver talents and is about to be sold into slavery, along with his family, when he cannot pay the debt (debt slavery was commonly practiced in Jesus's time). Falling on his knees, the servant begs, "Have patience with me, and I will pay you everything" (18:26). It's a ridiculous promise, given the enormity of the debt. A talent was worth more than fifteen years' wages of a laborer. You can work the math. For someone earning the common daily wage, repaying 10,000 talents would take 150,000 years (or only 30,000 years if he earned five times the common wage).

The debt was unpayable, and that is Jesus's point. It makes the king's response all the more shocking. Moved by pity, the king simply cancels the debt. He doesn't set up a payment plan. He doesn't demand any collateral. He forgives the entire amount.

As it happened, on his way out of the palace, the forgiven servant runs into a man who owes him the comparatively trifling sum of 100 denarii. Instead of extending the mercy that had been shown to him, the man demands to be paid in full and then throws his fellow debtor into prison. When the king finds out, it doesn't go well for debtor No. 1.

Being followers of Jesus means there is an expectation that we, too, forgive those who have wronged us. And here's the rub. That doesn't just mean small transgressions, like the cutting word said in jest or the inconsiderate act perpetrated out of ignorance. It is a call to radical forgiveness—a willingness not to define our enemies solely by an act so painful to us that the hurt may never completely go away. How do we forgive those who betray or abandon us, scourge us with their words, or abuse us or those we love? How do we begin to forgive those who take the life of someone we love? How could Holocaust survivors manage to forgive Nazis? How could the Mother Emanuel AME Church in Charleston, South Carolina, forgive the white supremacist who murdered nine of their fellow believers during a Bible study? We are moved by such acts of extraordinary mercy, but we may fairly wonder: How? How do we claim the self-sacrificing love that involves taking up the cross of radical forgiveness?

HOW?

In an old but familiar story I rediscovered recently, a Dutch woman named Corrie ten Boom[5] explained how she was able to forgive those who sent her to a concentration camp during World War II. She and her family were part of the resistance against the Nazis. They harbored Jews in their home until they could be ushered to safety. In 1944, Corrie and her family were caught. She and her sister Betsie were sent to Ravensbrück, where Betsie died. Corrie was released on a clerical error ten days before all of the other women her age were murdered.

In 1947, she had traveled from Holland to speak to a church in Germany and offer words of comfort and forgiveness. She said to the crowd, "When we confess our sins, God casts them into the deepest ocean. Gone forever." As people were leaving the church gathering, she spotted one of her tormentors from the camps. Not recognizing her, he approached, extended his hand and said, "How good it is to know that, as you say, all our sins are at the bottom of the sea!"

Her blood ran cold as he said, "I was a guard [at Ravensbrück], but since that time I have become a Christian. I know that God has forgiven me for the cruel things I did there, but I would like to hear it from your lips as well." As he stuck out his hand again, he asked, "Will you forgive me?"

As Corrie recalled, that request involved the hardest thing she had ever done. She did not feel like forgiving in that moment. But she also knew that forgiveness is not an emotion. It's an action, an imposition of the will. So she prayed silently, "Jesus help me. I can lift my hand...You supply the feeling." Though it was forced, as she reached out her hand toward the guard's, and as they touched, she said something remarkable happened. A healing warmth raced down her arm and flooded her entire being, bringing her to tears. "I forgive you, brother! With all my heart!" Corrie said that she had never experienced God's love so intensely as she did in that moment.

There are times when, even though we know we are called to forgive, we struggle when it involves someone who has done us great harm. Yet sometimes our most painful experiences can be catalysts to bring healing to others (and ourselves). A friend of mine who survived an abusive marriage is now a counselor for battered women. As a child, a man in our congregation was badly injured and his parents were killed when a drunk driver crashed into their car. That experience inspired him to become a pediatric orthopedic surgeon. Corrie ten Boom said she witnessed firsthand that those who were able to forgive went on to rebuild their lives. Those who could not let go of their bitterness became emotional invalids.

Still, there's the question of *how*. We sometimes wonder if we could offer the same kind of forgiveness if we experienced such harm, especially if the one who harmed us remains unrepentant. For the victims of unrepentant violence and abuse, who struggle with forgiving their abusers in the midst of unfathomable pain, Jesus's prayer offers an empowering option for them as they witness his own human struggle on the cross. Instead of saying "I forgive you," Jesus presents faithful Christians with an alternative response commensurate with Luke 6:28 ("Pray for those who abuse you"). In *praying for* his tormentors, Jesus's action becomes not an impossible example for victims to emulate, but a model for those who are wrongly wounded to regain their agency.[6] Sometimes in our struggle, amid our pain, the best we can do is to pray for those who injured us—to let ourselves believe that, even though their sin may have been conscious and premeditated, just as Jesus's killers knew they were killing him, they did not truly understand the import of their actions.

This does not mean that Jesus absolves us of the disciple's call to radical forgiveness. It also does not mean that we must become doormats for those who perpetrate harm. While we might be required to forgive those who are repentant, we are not required to, nor should we, subject ourselves to continuing mistreatment or abuse. Sometimes "adopting a prayerful stance at a distance"[7] is the best (or only) recourse. I want to be clear: If you are in an abusive situation, remove yourself from it as soon as is safely possible. Forgiveness does not mean that you submit yourself to further abuse; it means you do not allow past hurts to control or define your life, just as you are willing not to let another person's transgression against you forever define the totality of who they are.

During this season of Lent, when we practice self-sacrifice in remembrance of Jesus's journey to the cross, I invite you to practice the difficult discipline of forgiveness. First, think of someone you need to forgive. If forgiving is difficult for you, try praying for that person. And pray for the ability to act in a way that is forgiving. In my own life, I've found that it's hard to stay angry with someone when you're praying for them. Not surprisingly, I've also found that I'm not as good as Jesus. Sometimes, anger and bitterness, even when I thought I had completely let them go, rear their ugly heads again, and I have to keep praying and offering forgiveness as many times as "seventy times seven." Forgiveness is not always once and forever done for us, the way it is for Jesus. But it can get better and better until forgiveness is complete.

If you feel guilt or shame about your past, if you haven't asked for forgiveness, do so, and live in a way that reflects that your life is different because Jesus has already forgiven you, liberated you, and empowered you. And if you struggle to extend forgiveness to someone, remember the astronomical, inconceivable, unpayable debt that the king canceled on our behalf, as people who still participate in Jesus's crucifixion. Remember, too, that Jesus opened the door to a redeemed world where reconciliation prevails over vengeance, love prevails over hate, and mercy is inseparable from justice—and that he opened it with the simple words, "Father, forgive them; for they do not know what they are doing."

Today You Will Be with Me in Paradise

Chapter 2

TODAY YOU WILL BE WITH ME IN PARADISE

Then [the criminal] said, "Jesus, remember me when you come into your kingdom." He replied, "Truly I tell you, today you will be with me in Paradise."

Luke 23:42-43

It is the day of Jesus's death. He has already been sentenced to execution along with two other men Luke describes as "criminals," translated from Greek words meaning "evil workers" or "wrongdoers." Matthew's and Mark's Gospels call them "bandits." Above Jesus's head is posted an inscription, a mocking statement, attesting to his conviction of treason: "The King of the Jews." As Jesus hangs in agony from the cross, the religious leaders, the crowds, and the soldiers who have carried out the gruesome task of nailing him to the cross scoff at and mock him, saying: "He saved others; let him save himself if he is the Messiah" and "If you are the King of the Jews, save yourself!" (Luke 23:35, 37). *IF* you are the Messiah...*IF* you are the Son of God!

To the crowd, Jesus certainly doesn't look like any messiah they could ever imagine. What kind of messiah dies like a common criminal? What kind of king with the power to drive out the Romans gets captured and executed by the Romans? What kind of Son of God is allowed by his all-powerful Father to endure a painful, humiliating death like this? And, maybe more to the point of this passage and this chapter, what kind of man, witnessing this spectacle as he is dying alongside Jesus, still professes that Jesus is a king with an imperishable kingdom?

THE TEMPTATION IN THE WILDERNESS OF GOLGOTHA

The crowds may not have comprehended Jesus's identity. But Jesus knew. And he knew what he could do. Even then, Jesus had the power to do what the taunters dared him to do: free himself from the cross, defeat the Roman soldiers ordered to carry out his execution, and prove to the skeptics that he was unmistakably the Anointed One, the King.

The scene carries us back to Jesus's temptation in the wilderness. Just before he begins his public ministry, Mark briefly tells us (Mark 1:12-13) that Jesus is confronted by Satan (literally, "the adversary"). Luke's expansion of this story calls the tempter the devil (or "slanderer"), who challenges Jesus: "If"—there's that word again— "If you are the Son of God, command this stone to become a loaf of bread" (Luke 4:3). For someone fasting and hungry, the temptation to alleviate his physical suffering is obvious, but Jesus resists.

Jesus's adversary tries a different tack: If you will worship me, I will give you all the kingdoms of the world (4:6-7, paraphrased). Again, for someone who came to draw the world to God, having that kind of political power must have been at least a little tempting (as it is for some Christians today). Again, Jesus holds out.

Finally, the devil takes him to the highest point of the Temple in Jerusalem, which overlooked a deep valley. "If you are the Son of God," the adversary says, "throw yourself down from here, for it is written, / 'He will command his angels... / to protect you'" (4:9-10). What a sight that would have been! People all over Jerusalem would have either seen it or soon heard about it—this miraculous sign from God—and they would have worshipped Jesus as the Messiah. Here, too, there are obvious reasons why this temptation is, well, tempting.

Jesus doesn't take the bait. Instead, he responds to the tempter's misappropriation of scripture by quoting scripture himself. To the temptation to turn stone into bread, he replies: "It is written, 'One does not live by bread alone'" (4:4)—indicating that he puts his whole trust in God. To the second temptation, he responds, "Worship the Lord your God, / and serve only him" (4:8)—indicating that his full allegiance is to God and not to earthly power. And to the third temptation, a foreshadowing of the temptation he will experience from the cross, he tells the Adversary, "It is said, 'Do not put the Lord your God to the test'" (4:12). Then, Luke reports, "When the devil had finished every test, he departed from [Jesus] until an opportune time" (4:13).

It appears that Jesus's crucifixion *is* that opportune time. The tempter this time isn't the devil in the flesh, but that's not an important detail; you may recall that Jesus rebukes Peter as Satan when the disciple says "God forbid" that Jesus be arrested and crucified (Matthew 16:21-23). In that moment, Jesus regards Peter as "a stumbling block" (v. 23), an impediment to carrying out his ultimate mission—a needless temptation to turn away from the path that would take him to the cross. In fact, it is immediately after this exchange that Jesus tells his disciples, "If any want to become my followers, let them deny themselves and take up their cross and follow me" (16:24).

23

Now, at the cross, the tempters are the religious leaders, passersby, and soldiers. Even one of the criminals being crucified alongside Jesus, whose voice eerily channels that of the Adversary, joins in the taunts: "Are you not the Messiah? Save yourself and us!" (Luke 23:39). The irony of their jeers is that Jesus *is* who *they* declare he is. In order to show his true identity—the Messiah, the Son of God—Jesus must choose *not* to save himself. He must stay true to his mission, carrying his cross to the end. He refuses to save himself in order to save others.

THE HEART OF THE SECOND CRIMINAL

While throngs hurl vicious taunts, one person listens in dismay—the second criminal. Is it possible that he has seen Jesus as crowds gathered around him in Jerusalem, teaching every day in the Temple, healing the sick? Maybe he has witnessed the excited crowds who greeted Jesus as he made his triumphal entry into Jerusalem earlier in the week. Perhaps he even was among those shouting, "Blessed is the king / who comes in the name of the Lord!" (Luke 19:38). This man—defined for us as a criminal, as if that is the entirety of his being—has at the very least heard of Jesus and his reputation. He has no doubt been privy to the whispers and hopes that Jesus might be the Messiah, the one sent to rescue Israel. This criminal has definitely seen the inscription over Jesus's head, and perhaps he remembers Jesus, now mocked as the "king of the Jews," saying that the kingdom of God had drawn near and was among them.

Having experienced the same barbaric treatment and physical agony of crucifixion, the man overhears Jesus's prayer: "Father, forgive them; for they do not know what they are doing." There is something about Jesus's demeanor that cuts to the heart of this man. In the midst of the cacophony of jeering voices, he has listened to Jesus's words and understands what others do not: that Jesus is innocent. The hopes that had been placed in him weren't blasphemous, treasonous, or misplaced. Not only that: Unlike Pilate, the religious leaders, and the other criminal, he understands that Jesus really is a king—and that Jesus's death on a cross will neither end his kingship nor keep his kingdom from coming.

At this moment of realization, the criminal cannot help but launch a defense of the wrongly convicted Messiah. To his cynical companion in death, he asserts: Do you not fear God, since you and I are under the same life sentence as this man? The difference is that we are getting what we deserve for our deeds, but this man has done nothing wrong (Luke 23:40-41, paraphrased).

The criminal, whose heart has been forever changed by Jesus, enacts in his rebuke Jesus's earlier imperative to his disciples: "If another disciple sins, you must rebuke the offender" (17:3). His actions exhibit the attributes of a true disciple. Hanging from the cross next to Jesus, in his last moments of life, he becomes a follower of the Messiah. He has no time to repent of his earlier deeds, but in following Jesus he has lived out the literal meaning of the term: he has turned around and pointed himself in a different direction.

And then, with great reverence and intimacy, he calls out to Jesus in a way that no one else ever does in Luke's Gospel; he calls the man hanging next to him by name. Others have called Jesus rabbi (or teacher), Master, Son of David, and even Lord. Luke surely wants us to notice that only this criminal simply calls him Jesus. And when we look more closely at Jesus's name, we may discover that the way the criminal addresses him can be understood both as a prayer and a declaration of faith.

WHAT'S IN JESUS'S NAME?

This deathbed disciple speaks a name that summons and expresses a world of meaning and hope for Jews. "Jesus" was a common name in first-century Galilee, but a name that held great promise. Perhaps your parents named you for a family member or other person of great character in hopes that you would follow in his or her footsteps. The same was true for Jesus, who received an important biblical name. In Greek, the language in which the New Testament was written, Jesus's name is *Iesous* (pronounced e-ay-soos). However, Iesous was a transliteration of a name passed down from Hebrew, the language of the Old Testament writers. In Hebrew the name is *Yeshua* (or in English, Joshua). Yeshua, Iesous, Joshua, and Jesus all have the same meaning: he saves.

As you may recall from the Exodus story in the Old Testament, Joshua becomes Moses's right-hand man. At the end of Moses's life, after the Israelites have wandered in the wilderness for forty years, Joshua is bequeathed the mantle of responsibility of showing faith so that the people will trust God to lead them into the Promised Land. Joshua, aptly named, plays a key role in saving God's people. Just as admiring American parents in the nineteenth century often named children for George Washington or Benjamin Franklin, Jewish parents in Jesus's day expressed their hopes for the future by naming their sons Yeshua for the one God chose to deliver Israel from its oppressors.

Thus the name Jesus was wildly popular. Archaeologists have discovered seventy-one ossuaries engraved with the name Yeshua in burial caves near Jerusalem and dating from the time of Jesus's death. While many good Jewish parents hoped that a savior would rise from their children's generation, Mary and Joseph receive a divine announcement that their son will definitely grow into the name chosen for him by God. An angel of the Lord instructs Joseph, "You are to name him Jesus, for he will save his people from their sins" (Matthew 1:21). When the criminal on the cross addresses Jesus by name, he is not simply being familiar with him; as what he says next makes clear, he is expressing his faith in Jesus the Rescuer.

JESUS, REMEMBER ME

Though not as explicit as Peter's declaration that Jesus is "the Messiah, the Son of the living God" (Matthew 16:16), the criminal's words, "Jesus, remember me when you come into your kingdom" (Luke 23:42), are no less powerful as a profession of faith. And while he is appealing to Jesus, whose very name means "he saves," this dying man asks to be remembered instead of to be saved. Why?

Here again, there's more in these words than we might think at first. Asking to be remembered by God in itself is a request for deliverance or salvation—and also an appeal to God's promise. We find both the prayer and the promise throughout the Old Testament. God "remembers" Noah and all of the animals on the ark and delivers them from the flood (Genesis 8:1). God "remembers" the childless Rachel, and she conceives and gives birth to Joseph (30:22-24). God hears the cries of the Israelites in Egypt, remembers the covenant made with Abraham, and delivers them from slavery (Exodus 2:23-25). The psalmist writes, "Be mindful of your mercy, O LORD, and of your steadfast love.... / Do not remember the sins of my youth or my transgressions; / according to your steadfast love remember me, / for your goodness' sake, O LORD!" (Psalm 25:6-7). In the Eastern Orthodox tradition, funeral services include a hymn, "Memory Eternal," whose title may translate better into English as "The Eternal One Remembers." It is an appeal to God to remember the loved one who is being commended to God for eternity, and it is a strong echo of the dying criminal's request.

Yet this is more than just a request. It is a remarkable profession of faith that Jesus is a king and that those who are crucifying him have no power over his kingdom. The criminal doesn't specifically ask to be saved, but his hope is in the name of the one who saves. His hope is that Jesus will set aside his transgressions and will remember him, not for his past actions, but according to the newly minted condition of his heart, and according to Jesus's steadfast love and mercy—the same mercy Jesus prays for God to show those ignorant of the consequences of their heinous behaviors. It is the same mercy and forgiveness Jesus describes as extended by the father of the prodigal son, who interrupts his son's words of contrition before they are fully formed or expressed, and calls for a celebration:[1] "This son of mine was dead and is alive again; he was lost and is found!" (Luke 15:24). This humble and contrite criminal has confidence in Jesus and his kingdom, and he hopes to be included in that kingdom whenever and however it comes to pass.

KINGDOM? PARADISE? TODAY?

Just what is the nature of this kingdom that the criminal is affirming? Where is it? Even today, Christians sometimes seem confused about these questions. But Jesus's own words point to the answer. As he often stated, the kingdom of heaven had come near. It is among you and within you, he tells the Pharisees (Luke 17:21). It was present as he healed the sick, fed the hungry, and ate with sinners.

Immediately after his temptation in the wilderness, where Jesus has clarified the type of Messiah he is to be, he reveals his mission in his hometown of Nazareth. In the synagogue worship service (4:16-21), he reads from the scroll the words of the prophet Isaiah: "The Spirit of the Lord is upon me, / because he has anointed me / to bring good news to the poor.../ to proclaim release to the captives,.../ to let the oppressed go free, / to proclaim the year of the Lord's favor" (compare to Isaiah's description of rescue in 43:1-7). Then Jesus says to the amazed congregation, "Today this scripture has been fulfilled in your hearing" (Luke 4:21). It is both a mission statement and a picture of the kingdom.

If the criminal hanging next to him has followed Jesus's ministry, or at least his time in Jerusalem, he may already have glimpsed this picture that Jesus reveals. When he says, "Remember me when you come into your kingdom" (23:42), the captive who will never again be free in this life is declaring his faith in a place where the poor receive good news that they are honored as God's beloved children, a place where hopeless prisoners find release, a place where God comes to the rescue of those who are lost. It is only fitting that some of Jesus's last words are to a soul in need of rescue—and that Jesus is faithful to his mission even as he hangs from a cross.

What would Jesus have meant by "Paradise"? Most of us immediately think of heaven, living in Christ's presence in the afterlife. That's true so far as it goes, but there is deeper significance to Paradise as well. *Paradise* comes from a Persian word denoting a garden or forest. It often described the king's garden. In the Greek translation of the Old Testament, the Septuagint, the Garden of Eden was described as Paradise, where God walked with Adam and Eve, and they were given responsibility for caring for the garden (Genesis 2:15). In the Creator's garden, they experienced an intimate relationship with God based on complete trust—the kind of relationship that God always intended for human beings. Revelation uses Paradise imagery to represent the state of perfect and lasting life with God (Revelation 21:1-4; 22:1-5). It's a place where God's home will be with human beings and "death will be no more" (21:4). As in the original garden, there's a special, fruit-producing tree, but instead of being forbidden, its leaves bring healing to the nations of the world.

While the Gospel of John doesn't mention the word *Paradise*, it is symbolically portrayed as Jesus is betrayed and arrested

(John 18:1-11) in a garden. He is laid in a garden tomb (19:41). When she arrives at the tomb on Easter morning, Mary Magdalene confuses Jesus with the gardener (20:15). In meeting the resurrected Christ, she walks in intimate relationship with The Gardener. So, Paradise could be described as the fruition of the kingdom of God where one is with Christ—in the presence of God.[2] When Jesus tells the criminal beside him that he will be with him in Paradise, he is alluding to God's garden, to the image of a new creation. Beginning today, Jesus promises, you will no longer be defined as a criminal crucified for his crimes. You will be a new creation, at home and in harmony with the Creator of the world.

The kingdom, this rescue, this Paradise, this experience of life lived in God's presence begins *today* for those who place their trust in Jesus. Over and over, Jesus makes clear that the good news of salvation is not *just* for the "sweet by and by." Salvation is not just what some would call "fire insurance" for life after death. It is here and now. It is what Jesus meant when he said he came so that people may have life and have it abundantly (John 10:10). As he tells his friend Martha, "I am the resurrection *and* the life" (11:25, emphasis added). Sometimes we can become so fixated about the promise of life after death that we miss the eternal life and Kingdom living into which Jesus invites the world here and now—today.

Theologian Eberhard Busch, professor emeritus of Reformed Theology at the University of Göttingen, Germany, states it this way, "This kingdom of God will not come in a remote future; it dawns already, now, 'today.' This is true because the ruler of the kingdom of God is already with you, in your life and in your dying."[3]

John Wesley once said salvation "is not a blessing which lies on the other side of death.... It is not something at a distance: it is a present thing, a blessing which, through the free mercy of God, ye are now in possession of,"[4] since Jesus's words reflected "you are saved," and "you have been saved." For Wesley, for the criminal on the cross, for you and me, the "salvation which is here spoken of might be extended to the entire work of God, from the first dawning of grace in the soul till it is consummated in glory."[5] And yet that is a concept that is difficult for some people to grasp, or to really believe.

Some years ago, a man I had known very well asked me to come to his bedside as he was dying. I was familiar with his past, which included multiple affairs and abandoning his wife and child for years in order to pursue a hedonistic lifestyle that led to issues related to addiction. His early adulthood years left a trail of pain and tears in their wake. However, he had also become a changed man. He became sober and later reconciled with his family. He was happy, outgoing, funny, and loved, but on his deathbed he was concerned. He said, "Susan, I've done some terrible things in my life, and I don't know if God can forgive all of that. Do you think I will be with Jesus when I die? Can God forgive what I've done?"

I said to him, "That forgiveness was offered 2,000 years ago on the cross." Although I already knew the answer to the question I posed, I asked it anyway: "Have you asked forgiveness for what you've done from God and from your family?"

"Yes, often" he replied. Then I said, "You may struggle with what you did in your past, but Jesus only remembers you as his beloved child."

Isn't that what we all want—to be remembered by God not for the worst things we ever did but according to God's steadfast love for us?

'REMEMBER ME' IS NOT JUST ABOUT US

The prophet Isaiah speaks a promise from God to people who thought God had abandoned and forgotten about them: "Can a woman forget her nursing child, / or show no compassion for the child of her womb? / Even these may forget, / yet I will not forget you. / See, I have inscribed you on the palms of my hands" (Isaiah 49:15-16a).

The Eternal One always remembers us. Nothing, as the apostle Paul put it, can separate us from the love of Christ: not death, not earthly powers, nor height, nor depth (Romans 8:37-39)—not even the worst things we have ever done. We cling to this "blessed assurance." We claim this promise for ourselves, as did one of the criminals who died next to Jesus.

But our journey to the cross is not complete if we focus too much on Jesus's free gift to us and not enough on the call to give of ourselves to others. Jesus "remembered" the penitent criminal. In imitating Christ as his disciples, we cannot allow ourselves to forget about those who have never truly experienced the love of God. Otherwise, we betray him just as surely as Judas; we deny Jesus just as shamefully as Peter.

The movie *Dead Man Walking* tells the story of Sister Helen Prejean, a nun who receives a request for a visit from an inmate on death row as his execution date draws near. The inmate, Matthew, has taken part in a brutal rape and double murder. There is no question of his guilt, even though he refuses to acknowledge his crime. After several visits, Sister Helen agrees to become Matthew's spiritual adviser. Gradually, she persuades him to take responsibility for what he did. In one of the film's most powerful scenes, he finally confesses his guilt to Sister Helen. When they pray together, she tells him, "You are a son of God, Matthew."

Matthew reacts to this good news of the gospel with a mixture of surprise, tears, and joy. "Nobody," he says, "ever called me no son of God before."[6]

Imagine the poverty and desolation of a life in which no one ever reminded you that you are a child of God—much less treated you with the basic dignity and fairness that is your birthright as someone made in God's image and likeness. Imagine how that might skew your view of life, of your own identity, and of your relationships with other people. Then imagine the life-changing, liberating effect of learning the good news that you are God's beloved, that God will never write you off, that the nails that pinned Jesus's arms to the cross testify to God's promise: "I have inscribed you on the palms of my hands."

If you can imagine all that, then you can begin to grasp the power of Jesus's words from the cross to the lost, the poor in spirit, those who feel all alone, those who carry crushing burdens of shame and guilt. Today, your sins are forgiven and your past is forgotten. Today, you're invited to a great feast given by the king himself. Today, you can participate in the abundant life of the kingdom that will never end. All of that and more is contained in those eight, spare words Jesus spoke as he struggled for breath: "Today you will be with me in Paradise."

That is the message that Jesus offered not just to the criminal alongside him, not just to me and you, but to the whole world. He calls us, as his disciples, to spread the word, not just verbally but in our actions toward others. Especially during Lent, we are invited to lean in and remember his mission statement: I came to bring good news to the poor and proclaim release to the captives—and then "go and do likewise" (Luke 10:37).

Bring light to those who sit in darkness. Bring comfort to those who are imprisoned by fear and grief. Bring a healing touch to those who are in pain. Be outlandishly generous friends to those for whom love is a stranger. In showing them a glimpse of God's kingdom in these ways, you extend Jesus's invitation to be with him in Paradise.

My God, My God

Chapter 3

My God, My God

When it was noon, darkness came over the whole land until three in the afternoon. At three o'clock Jesus cried out with a loud voice, "Eloi, Eloi, lema sabachthani?" which means, "My God, my God, why have you forsaken me?"

Mark 15:33-34

Have you ever seen a godforsaken place? I have. Such places take many forms: an abandoned ghost town in the West or somewhere that is remote, inhospitable, and largely devoid of life, like Death Valley in California or the Salt Flats of Utah. At first glance, we might be tempted to think that these places have been abandoned by God, who created the wastelands and trackless deserts as well as the beautiful beaches and lush forests.

People can feel godforsaken too. My guess is that all of us have experienced feeling as if we were abandoned by God at some point in our lives. I know I have. In the midst of terrible situations, I have wondered just where God was. I have asked whether God had somehow forgotten to show up when divine help was most wanted or needed. I've felt desolate, abandoned, and all alone. In other words, I've felt like Jesus felt as he was tortured, mocked, and dying on the cross.

I grew up as a "daddy's girl." Although I know this isn't everyone's experience, I enjoyed the distinct good fortune of having a tender, loving, doting father. He was always ready to listen, always forgiving, always there to wipe away a tear, offer a hug, and give advice, solicited or otherwise. His was a true expression of unconditional love. It was his love that made it easy for me to believe in a heavenly Father who was full of mercy and unconditional love. Needless to say, I adored my father.

For more than two years, my dad suffered from a protracted illness, one that we knew would eventually take his life. It was a physical and emotional roller coaster. There were times when he would feel well, experiencing only diminished energy, and it would seem perhaps that the doctors' terminal diagnosis might have been wrong. Then, without warning, there would be an emergency trip to the hospital, the family would be summoned, death appeared imminent, suffering abounded—and then, miraculously, a modest recovery would follow. With each successive cycle of decline and recovery, the physical suffering became worse—often unbearable. Gradually, our prayers shifted from asking for healing for my dad to begging God to mercifully end his suffering.

It was in this season nearest the end of his life when Dad's suffering was so acute that it became all of our suffering as a family. On one particularly despondent morning, I had a crying, ranting, fist-shaking conversation with God. I've read some of those conversations, which appear occasionally in the Psalms, but I never imagined myself in such a situation. I never thought I would allow those expressions to escape my lips for fear of being struck by lightning. But on this awful morning, it happened. I said: "God, we prayed that Daddy would be healed, and he wasn't. Then we prayed that he wouldn't suffer, but he has—terribly. Lord, I've prayed that you would take him, because it would be a blessing to him and to us, and yet he lingers in pain. Are you listening? Do you hear our prayers? Do you even care? I would love an answer, but I really don't expect one anymore!" Why had it seemed that God was falling down on the job of heavenly parenthood just when we needed help the most? Why had it seemed like the assurances of God's love and presence with us were just empty promises?

Sometimes we are afraid of expressing this type of raw honesty to God because we fear God will be offended (as if God didn't already know our thoughts and the feelings of our heart). Worse, perhaps, we wonder if what we are thinking could be true. Are we abandoned? Has God forsaken or forgotten us in our suffering? Is God even there?

If you have ever had these thoughts, if you have ever felt godforsaken, you are not alone. We can take comfort in knowing that even Jesus, the Word made flesh, fully human and fully divine, felt forsaken by God in the darkest moment of his earthly life. And he not only felt it: he spoke it for others—including us—to hear.

But did God abandon Jesus? Was Jesus left alone in his suffering? Even though he *felt* godforsaken, did he truly believe that he was abandoned? The last words Jesus speaks from the cross in the Gospels of Mark and Matthew are the darkest. However, if we carefully follow them to their conclusion, we will discover a much deeper richness to Jesus's words and to the story of the crucifixion. I believe we will find that they can represent for us some of the most hope-filled and life-giving words in all the Gospels. We need to hear these words from the context in which Jesus speaks them. Through his cry, we may encounter the hope Jesus intends for us to cling to in our darkest moments.

As church communities, national communities, and even a global community, we may find new reservoirs of trust in God's deliverance at times when it feels like the world is spiraling out of control and no longer operates under God's loving hand. As I write these words—amid a global pandemic that has taken hundreds of thousands of lives worldwide (later to surpass one million), disrupted countless other lives, inflicted hardship, hunger, and fear—it is understandable that many feel forsaken by God. It has happened at other times when it seemed that the world was falling apart, or even coming to an end. It happened amid the Black Death, the plague that wiped out one-third or more of the population of Europe in the mid-1300s. Within our own living memory, the awful events of September 11, 2001, led some to ask where God had been. Amid the unfathomable horror of Auschwitz, Elie Wiesel witnessed a trial staged by three rabbis. The defendant was God. In the end, the rabbis concluded that God was liable. Then, Wiesel said, the rabbis went to pray.[1]

As scripture records—including the scripture Jesus quoted from the cross—the people of Israel, the people whose very name means "struggles with God," felt at times that God had forsaken them. They didn't run from those feelings. Instead, they preserved their raw emotions in psalms that they sang together. They sang the psalmist's words about feeling surrounded by enemies: "There is no one who takes notice of me; / no refuge remains to me; / no one cares for me" (Psalm 142:4b). They sang about the experience of being exiled in Babylon, after the Temple, which they believed was God's home among them, had been destroyed (Psalm 137). They sang about their feelings of distress: "My tears have been my food / day and night, / while people say to me continually, / 'Where is your God?'" (42:3).

When the people sang these songs in worship, they were being painfully honest about their feelings. And why not? After all, God already knew what was on their hearts. But as we will see, the songs did not end with feelings of hopelessness. There was more to the story in those psalms. There was more to Jesus's story than the psalmist's words of despair that he spoke as he struggled to breathe. There is more to our individual story too. There is more to our community's story. And just as the rabbi-jurors at Auschwitz prayed to the God they had just put on trial, when we follow the story of Jesus's words to its conclusion, we may find that our own worst trials, our moments of deepest despair and isolation, take us back to God.

JESUS IS HUMAN TOO

Golgotha—The Skull—already felt like a godforsaken place to people in Jerusalem. It was a place associated with torture, suffering, and death. Every time crucifixions took place there, it was a reminder of the power and cruelty of their enemies. Even if you didn't personally witness a crucifixion, simply to stand on Golgotha was to feel as if you were on haunted ground.

His words tell us that Jesus felt it too. Even before the nails were driven into his hands and the crossbeam that held him was hoisted into place, the emotional and physical pain he had already endured was considerable. He had been betrayed by Judas, one of his own chosen disciples. According to Matthew's and Mark's Gospels, all of Jesus's friends except Peter had run away as soon as he was arrested. As for Peter, the most outspokenly zealous disciple, he denied even knowing Jesus, not just once but three times. Jesus endured being condemned as a blasphemer by the religious leaders of his own people. Then, adding injury to insult, he was mocked by the soldiers, stripped of his clothes, and severely beaten before making the final walk to his execution.

In Roman times, a person condemned to crucifixion, already weakened from torture and the blood loss of flogging, was required to carry the heavy crossbeam to the place of execution. This was true for Jesus. His beating may have been especially severe, considering that the soldiers forced Simon of Cyrene (Mark 15:21)—a Jewish pilgrim from present-day Libya who had come to Jerusalem for the Passover—to help carry the crossbeam.

Once Jesus arrived at Golgotha, he would have been suffering from pain, shock, dehydration, and loss of blood. Then, his hands and feet would have been nailed to the cross and affixed in such a way as to cause a slow death. Jesus and the two men beside him would have had to attempt to hold themselves up by the strength in their legs in order to avoid suffocation. As the day went on, Jesus, already weakened from the flogging, would have struggled to breathe as his strength began to fail. The few words he uttered from the cross would have been very difficult to speak. Victims of crucifixion ultimately died from asphyxiation when they could no longer hold themselves up; that is why the soldiers, ready to be done with their duty before sundown, broke the legs of the two men hanging beside Jesus so they would die. While Jesus hung on the cross for six hours—I invite you to imagine what those six hours must have felt like—some victims endured for much longer.

Crucifixion was designed to create the greatest amount of humiliation and physical suffering for the condemned in order to set an example for others, so as to keep the Pax Romana—the peace of Rome—and deter those who witnessed it from committing sedition or inspiring rebellion against the state. Just as brutal lynchings of Black men and women in the United States were perpetrated to terrorize communities of color into silence and submission—Black Christians have long understood the connection between the cross and the lynching tree—Roman crucifixions are accurately seen as acts of state terror. They were intended to leave cowed onlookers feeling helpless and hopeless against the power of the empire, so that they might think that not even God could deliver them.

Scripture tells us that for three hours, from noon until 3 p.m., darkness covered the entire land. This was certainly the darkest hour in Jesus's life. It was also the darkest hour in human history. It was as deep as the darkness of the formless void in creation before God speaks light into existence (Genesis 1:1-2). It was as dense as the plague of fog and darkness that covered the land of Egypt for three days as God attempts to convince Pharaoh to release God's people from slavery (Exodus 10:21-29). It was as dark as the belly of the great fish in which the prophet Jonah is entombed for three days as he ponders his deliverance from death in a watery grave and the redemptive work to which God calls him (Jonah 1:17-3:2).

In the midst of his pain, humiliation, and suffering, in the agony of this darkness, Jesus turns to prayer. This is his regular practice, as the Gospels attest. In Galilee, he would seek times when he could escape the crowds that flocked to him so he could go off to an isolated place and pray. He refers to the Temple in Jerusalem not as a house of worship but a house of prayer. His last act before his arrest is to lead his disciples out from their gathering in the upper room and through the Kidron Valley to pray on the Mount of Olives.

So it is natural that Jesus's last words from the cross include a prayer. From his lips pour forth the opening words of Psalm 22, addressed to God in his native Aramaic tongue, "Eloi, Eloi, lema sabachthani?" Matthew and Mark translate the words for us: "My God, my God, why have you forsaken me?" In their Gospels these are the only words Jesus speaks from the cross. They obviously reflect the depth of his human suffering and pain.

Earlier in Mark's Gospel, we hear another prayer issued from Jesus's lips, one addressed to God in more intimate, familial language. As he kneels in the Garden of Gethsemane, contemplating what lies ahead, Jesus prays to his heavenly parent, "Abba, Father, for you all things are possible; remove this cup from me; yet, not what I want, but what you want" (Mark 14:36). In the depths of Jesus's humanity, he, like any of us would, wishes to avoid the pain and suffering of the cross, and yet he also surrenders the outcome of the coming moments into the hands of his heavenly Father. Your will be done, he says, not mine.

In this moment on the cross, Jesus's prayer appears to have gone unanswered. The cup has not been removed. The suffering and pain become his unwanted companion. Feeling forsaken, Jesus moves from the intimate language of child to parent, to the common address of all humanity, "My God."[2] But why would Jesus, who is also divine, feel abandoned by God? Isn't he part of the Trinity? Shouldn't he be above asking if God has abandoned him? While I think that these words are difficult for us to hear, they also are some of the most endearing words of Jesus because they most clearly reveal his humanity. In this moment, he is just like us—not simply in that he was born and walked on this earth, not simply in that he shared our human physical needs for food, water, sleep, and shelter. In this moment, he is also like us in that he feels what we have all felt: humiliation, betrayal, pain, suffering, abandonment— godforsakenness. Like the people of Israel, like the psalmists at times, he is struggling with God. That's why we need to lean in and listen to his words closely. For now, it is important to note that Jesus doesn't deny God's existence. He does not turn away from the God who seems to have abandoned him. Instead, he turns *toward* God as he asks, If you are there, God, why haven't you come to help me?

IS THE LORD AMONG US OR NOT?

It must have taken a great deal of effort for Jesus to speak these few words from Psalm 22. Had he continued to the next verses of the psalm, he would have said aloud what we have sometimes felt: "Why are you so far from helping me, from the words of my groaning? /

O my God, I cry by day, but you do not answer; / and by night, but find no rest" (22:1b-2).

Have you or someone you know ever uttered or thought these sentiments? Perhaps after a difficult medical diagnosis, the betrayal of a friend or spouse, or amid the throes of debilitating pain? Maybe after some senseless tragedy? I have. For me, that's part of my human condition. Experiencing times when I feel godforsaken is part of what it means to be human. And that, I believe, is one reason Jesus utters these words of despair. He knows that his story does not end on the cross. He has already told his disciples more than once, as they later recalled, that he would be handed over to the authorities and be killed and would be raised on the third day. He understands that the cross is merely a way station on his journey (and ours). But he quotes the psalmist because he wants us to know he understands our pain and suffering, and our questioning, because his human experience has plumbed the complete depths of our own. When life takes us to dark valleys of despair and isolation, if we're listening to Jesus's words from the cross, he is reminding us that he has already been there. He has traveled through the same godforsaken wilderness. We may feel abandoned, but we are never alone.

The feeling of being forsaken by God in the middle of God's delivering work is not unique to us, Jesus, or the psalmist. As I noted earlier, the Israelites experienced this same feeling on multiple occasions; one in particular stands out to me. During their enslavement in Egypt, God puts on a spectacular display of ten plagues to convince Pharaoh to set God's people free (Exodus 7–11). They have already seen God's mighty acts, and yet even before they cross the Red Sea, they panic when they see Pharaoh's chariots kicking up dust on the horizon, and they want to go back to their old lives of oppression. Then, after personally witnessing God's mightiest act of deliverance, they still have not learned to trust in God. Their feet are barely finished crossing through the parted waters of the Red Sea when they hit the wilderness of the Sinai Desert. Their water runs out. The people are parched, and they complain to Moses, "'Why did you bring us out of Egypt, to kill us and our children and livestock with thirst?'...'Is the LORD among us or not?'" (17:3, 7b).

In some form or fashion, it's a question we probably ask too. Is this Lord among us or not?

I write these words at a time that has brought mind-boggling change and disruption on national and global levels. Our world has been overwhelmed by a lethal pandemic that continues to threaten the lives of millions. As we wait for the development of a vaccine and better treatment options, most of us remain sheltered—and unusually isolated—behind closed doors. We are also discovering that the plague of racism, a human-made sickness that many of us let ourselves believe was in decline, is still raging and has proven more deadly than many had ever understood.

Early in the COVID-19 crisis, there were reports of empty grocery store shelves and people hoarding toilet paper (of all things). As I write this, laundry bleach and hand sanitizer are still scarce. I saw a picture on the news one day of people fighting over bottled water in a grocery store, as if their home taps might stop working in a pandemic. One friend posted a picture on Facebook with the tongue-in-cheek caption: "Waiting, yelling, and fighting with friends here at Costco. It's nutty!" Thankfully, he managed to maintain a sense of humor through others' fears and anxieties that the coronavirus has brought.

For some reason, many have become fearful that there will not be enough water or food to take care of their physical needs. While it's good to take precautions during this time, it's as if they, like the Israelites in wilderness, have no trust that God is among them, that

God hears their cries, or that God cares about what happens to them. Perhaps they worry that they are on their own, that they will wake up one morning abandoned, alone, and thirsty. Our faith tells us that we are never alone or abandoned. While God has given us the intellect to plan and make wise decisions, we never have to be afraid that we have been abandoned by the God who provides for our needs.

That brings me back to the story of the Israelites in the apparently waterless wilderness. Moses, following God's instructions, strikes a rock with his staff, and out pours water to quench the thirst of the wandering Israelites. God hears. God cares. God *is* among them. God hears. God cares. God is among us too.

HEARING GOD SPEAK

When my father was in his last weeks of life, as I finished my fist-shaking rant at God—"Are you listening? Do you hear our prayers? Do you even care? I would love an answer, but I really don't expect one anymore!"—I headed to the gym, got on the stair-climber exercise machine, and angrily began burning off some steam. I felt that God had abandoned my dad and our family. I had taken my Bible along to multitask, planning to read and study while I exercised. When I opened it, a little piece of paper fluttered out from between the pages. I grabbed it as it floated toward the floor. It was a page I had torn from an Upper Room devotional book and stuck in my Bible about a year earlier. The reading for that day, a passage I had completely forgotten from Isaiah 49, was an answer to my prayer. I included a portion of it in the previous chapter of this book. It's worth quoting at greater length here, because it contains the words of God addressed to people who felt abandoned and forsaken during the Babylonian exile:

Sing for joy, O heavens, and exult, O earth;
> *break forth, O mountains, into singing!*
For the LORD has comforted his people,
> *and will have compassion on his suffering ones.*

But Zion said, "The LORD has forsaken me,
> *my Lord has forgotten me."*
Can a woman forget her nursing child,
> *or show no compassion for the child of her womb?*
Even these may forget,
> *yet I will not forget you.*
See, I have inscribed you on the palms of my hands.
> *Isaiah 49:13-16a*

There on the stair climber, my heart was melted by the love and comfort of God. What I learned later was that, while I might have been ready for my dad to go, he was not—but God brought comfort and peace in those last days as we said our final I love yous and as we heard Dad say his last words, "I'm goin' home. I'm goin' home."

Since that time, even though I have had moments where I did not sense God's presence, I never again doubted God's presence, God's love, or whether God hears our prayers, because of the God who became flesh, on whose palms our names are inscribed, and who died for us while we were yet sinners.

JESUS AND THE REST OF THE STORY

Even though Jesus *feels* abandoned in his suffering, humiliation, and humanity, he *knows* that he is truly not alone. Until Isaiah reminded me on that exercise machine, I had forgotten the scripture passages of God's compassion and care for God's suffering ones. But Jesus remembers the rest of the story. Jesus remembers all of the words of the psalm that he began to pray from the cross, the song that he needed to carry him through in hope in his final moments of life. He wants us to hear them, even if he didn't recite them all.

If I begin the words to a song that we all know, I'll bet you can fill in the next line. "Jesus loves me this I know" ("for the Bible tells me so"). Or "Amazing grace, how sweet the sound" ("that saved a wretch like me"). Or "This little light of mine" ("I'm gonna let it shine"). Similarly, Jesus knew the Psalms backward and forward. During his ministry, he quoted from them regularly. And so did his Jewish friends, because they sang them in synagogue and at home. Jesus, in his suffering, might feel forsaken by God in that awful moment, but he knows that the song does not end on that note of despair. If he had had the strength to keep singing Psalm 22, some in the crowd might have joined in: "In you our ancestors trusted" ("they trusted, and you delivered them"). "To you they cried, and were saved" ("in you they trusted, and were not put to shame") (from vv. 4-5). Jesus knows that God heard the cries of the Israelites enslaved in Egypt and delivered them from death. He knows that God heard their cries in the wilderness and delivered them from hunger and thirst. Jesus knows that God heard the cries of those in Babylon and, like a nursing mother, brought comfort to God's children.

Jesus does not have to quote the rest of the psalm because he knows that his followers will understand the reference and he wants them to remember how the song continues: "On you I was cast from my birth, / and since my mother bore me you have been my God" (v. 10). "For he did not despise or abhor / the affliction of the afflicted; / he did not hide his face from me, / but heard when I cried to him" (v. 24). Finally, Jesus knows and trusts in the One who is declared in the end of the psalm, "To him, indeed, shall all who sleep in the earth bow down; / before him shall bow all who go down to the dust, / and I shall live for him.... / Future generations will be told about the Lord, / and proclaim his deliverance to a people yet unborn, / saying that he has done it" (vv. 29-31). This psalm, Jesus's last words from the cross, is not a song about being forsaken forever. It is a song of triumph.

TRUSTING IN THE ONE WHO NEVER ABANDONS OR FORSAKES US

Jesus knew the end of the song. He knew the entire arc of God's saving actions in history. In his humanity he trusted, even in his darkest moment, in the One who didn't feel near, but who he knew would deliver him, so that future generations would come to know the power of his deliverance; so that future generations would come to live in that power and be delivered from their own sin, fears, and doubts. That is the message for us on our own personal journey. It is the message for our worshipping communities. And it the message for a world where fear, mistrust, and despair so often tear people apart and leave them isolated.

In the midst of our suffering and trials, God in Jesus Christ is with us, hearing our cries, walking through the darkness, and leading us into the light and victory. On the other side of our Good Fridays, Easter is always waiting.

It is all a matter of our perspective, of our ability to trust in God through the end. Maybe in church you've sung the old hymn, "There Is a Balm in Gilead." But have you ever looked up the scripture that inspired it? It comes from Jeremiah, who is sometimes called "the weeping prophet." Jeremiah's ministry took place as the Babylonian invaders threatened and ultimately destroyed Jerusalem. Gilead was a hilly, green land east of the Jordan River that was known for trees whose sap was used as a healing balm. Jeremiah does not invoke this image to comfort the people; instead, he writes words of despair:

> *My joy is gone, grief is upon me,*
> *my heart is sick.*

Hark, the cry of my poor people
from far and wide in the land:
"*Is the LORD not in Zion?*
Is her King not in her?"...
"*The harvest is past, the summer is ended,*
and we are not saved."
For the hurt of my poor people I am hurt. . . .

Is there no balm in Gilead?
Is there no physician there?
Why then has the health of my poor people
not been restored?

Jeremiah 8:18-22

The hymn takes the opposite tack: Yes, there *is* a balm in Gilead. Yes, there *is* a physician. Yes, the Lord *is* in Zion. Yes, God remembers us. What makes this faith statement even more powerful is that "There Is a Balm in Gilead," an African American spiritual, was sung by a community that was experiencing racial violence, oppression, and discrimination that seemed like they would never end. But they believed that the story would end not in despair but victory, because they knew that God in the human person of Jesus had walked their road ahead of them and triumphed over hatred and death.

Jesus wants us to lean in and hear his last words that we may experience the same hope that he had in God, his heavenly Father, who time after time heard the cries of Israel, offered comfort, and delivered them.

CARING FOR THE ABANDONED AND FORGOTTEN

As we listen to understand the context of Jesus's words, they also become an inspiration to follow his example of caring for those who feel abandoned or forgotten. These words are not just meant to reassure us. They are meant to challenge us, to remind us that, here on earth, we are Jesus's hands and feet. We are called to reach out to those who feel that hope is lost, who feel that God has forsaken them, and show them that they are not alone.

Jesus could never see need or suffering without turning to help. Countless times he had compassion for and healed the sick, the lame, and the blind. He fed the hungry and welcomed and ate with those the rest of the world deemed outcasts. Like Simon of Cyrene, we are called to help carry a cross that others cannot bear alone. Have you ever wondered why Simon, a person never mentioned anywhere else in the Bible, is known by name to the Gospel writers? Me too. Mark's Gospel contains a clue. It identifies Simon as the father of Alexander and Rufus. Why would that detail be important unless Alexander and Rufus were known to early Christian communities? Paul's Letter to the Romans offers another tantalizing clue. In his greetings to the believers, he mentions Rufus and Rufus's mother, who he says was a mother to him too. Could this Rufus be the son of the man who carried Jesus's cross? Could Simon have been standing in the crowd on that fateful day because he had become a follower of Jesus? We can never know for sure. What we can know is that Mark wants us to understand that we, as Jesus's disciples, must carry Jesus's cross on behalf of others who are struggling. In that sense, the cross is not a burden but an opportunity.

The months of pandemic and racial reckoning have given us as followers of Christ the opportunity to show our neighbors that they have not been forsaken by God. The church that I serve—and I expect it's true of your church too—has prepared ways to stay connected to those in our community who are sheltered in nursing homes and hospitals, whom we are not allowed to see in person.

Isn't it amazing the ways in which we have become creative with FaceTime, Zoom, and even the simple telephone?

While we may be isolated, COVID-19 has given us the chance to show the love of our neighbors in new ways. In embracing that opportunity, we may hear stories of loneliness, job insecurity, fear, and anxiety. We may encounter hungry, frightened children who depended on their now closed schools for breakfast and lunch and summer community programs. We may reach out with Meals on Wheels to older adults who are homebound, isolated, and unable to cook for themselves. We may find ourselves listening to our brothers and sisters as they tell us of the deep injury they experienced (and continue to experience) simply because of the color of their skin—and come to grips with the truth that racism denies the sovereignty of God. If we follow the way of the cross, we will encounter those along our road who are sick and suffering, those who ask the all-too-human question, "God, why have you forsaken me?"

By walking along with them, by helping to carry their burden, we have an opportunity to remind them how the psalm ends—not with isolation, but with Easter. Through our actions, we help deliver the good news: God is here; you are not forgotten. Suffering does not get to have the last word. Human fear and violence do not get the last word. Love has the last word. Pick up someone's cross and be the message.

Woman,
Here Is
Your Son

Chapter 4

WOMAN, HERE IS YOUR SON

Meanwhile, standing near the cross of Jesus were his mother, and his mother's sister, Mary the wife of Clopas, and Mary Magdalene. When Jesus saw his mother and the disciple whom he loved standing beside her, he said to his mother, "Woman, here is your son." Then he said to the disciple, "Here is your mother." And from that hour the disciple took her into his own home.

John 19:25b-27

A s I write this book, the world looks very different from the one I inhabited just a few months earlier. The global pandemic that at this point has killed, in growing numbers, hundreds of thousands of people around the world has disrupted almost every facet of life here. Each day, it seems, a new space or community in which we lived and navigated is sealed off due to COVID-19, and we have to become creative in finding new ways to do or access old things.

In the spring of 2020, colleges and universities pivoted to online learning experiences. Elementary students accessed their teachers via laptops the schools had sent home with them. Instead of broadcasting from a studio with a live audience, late-night comedy show hosts came to us from a room in their homes or even their backyards. Instead of gathering at church, people met for worship or Bible study screen-to-screen by way of Zoom or Google Meet. Attending church from the comfort of our den, wearing pajamas and drinking coffee, became commonplace. Instead of inviting friends into their homes, people organized socially distanced get-togethers outside. Take-out meals became "bring-out" meals as restaurant staff carried your food to your vehicle after you phoned them to let them know you had arrived. Never in my wildest dreams did I *ever, ever, ever* imagine taking the place of my husband's barber, but it happened.

Out of necessity, families adopted new ways of being too. Spread out across the country, aunts, uncles, and cousins who, in the days before the pandemic, might have seen each other in person only infrequently discovered they could have group conversations every week with Zoom get-togethers. Friends began scheduling regular Zoom social hours that, for many, became a high point of their week.

In ways like these, the upheaval that has disrupted so many lives so dramatically and injuriously—leaving millions of Americans unemployed, lacking food security, and threatened with the prospect of eviction from their homes or apartments—also has opened up new possibilities with the potential to change our lives for the better, if we are open to them, if we are willing to change. I think of a visit that Robert Kennedy made to South Africa in 1966, against the wishes of the apartheid government of that country, after receiving an invitation to address students in Cape Town on their university's "Day of Reaffirmation of Academic and Human Freedom." In his memorable speech, Kennedy challenged the students to work for change. The world, he told them, "cannot be moved by those who cling to a present which is already dying." An ancient Chinese saying, "May he live in interesting times," was intended as a curse, he noted. "Like it or not we live in interesting times. They are times of danger and uncertainty; but they are also the most creative of any time in the history of mankind."[1]

Like it or not, we live in "interesting" times. They leave us with question after question. Will people whose lives have been disrupted and demolished physically or financially ever be the same? How will our most vulnerable fare in the midst of this pandemic? Will we be able to find the courage, strength of voice, and means necessary to create a safe place for them, and to create a better, less vitriolic, less polarized world? Will we allow the interiors of our collective hearts to be remodeled in a way that finally acknowledges the sacred worth of all of God's children regardless of the color of their skin, social or economic status, or sexual orientation?

In life we are continually required to find new ways to do and access old ways of being. We continually wonder how we will navigate the challenges that lie ahead of us. We often wonder if our lives can be the way we imagine or the way God imagines life for us.

I suspect that, once the pandemic subsides, we, as churches, will not go back reflexively and strictly to the way things were before. It's not that communal worship in a shared physical space will go away. But there are likely to be exciting new, complementary options: live, online services that allow people anywhere in the world to share the same worship experience; Zoom Bible studies and discussion groups that can draw people in from all over the community; services in which people can take part in Holy Communion—from fifty locations at once.

Jesus's words, spoken from the cross in the Gospel of John, present us with a lens through which to consider these questions and musings, and they offer an invitation into a new way of being.

As Jesus tenderly speaks directly to two of the dearest people in his life, his mother and one of his closest friends and disciples, he offers us a glimpse of hope for the days ahead and a new way to access and accomplish the life and world God imagines. How could Jesus possibly have conveyed all that in the simple words, "Woman, here is your son"? Keep reading.

STAYING NEAR THE CROSS

Among Jesus's followers, the Gospels focus most of their attention on the twelve men Jesus called to follow him. But it's also clear from these texts that many others traveled with Jesus during his ministry, and women were always part of that group; some of them, Luke tells us, even helped pay for expenses using their own resources. So it's understandable that women would be among those who were with Jesus during his final hours.

All four Gospels mention women who were brave enough to follow Jesus to the cross and witness his crucifixion. It's easy to imagine their desire to stay near the cross to demonstrate to Jesus that he was not alone, and to be near their friend, teacher, and Lord to hear his last words. The women's names and number vary from Gospel to Gospel. That's not surprising since Matthew and Luke tell us that there were a number of women who followed the procession from inside the city walls out to Golgotha, and Matthew makes clear that he is not attempting to list all of them. John's Gospel mentions four (John 19:25): Mary the wife of Clopas; Mary Magdalene; Jesus's aunt (referenced only as "his mother's sister"); and one named only in terms of her relationship to Jesus, "his mother" (whose name we know from the other Gospels but that John does not mention).

The last time we saw Jesus's mother in the Fourth Gospel was in chapter 2, at the beginning of his ministry. Jesus and his disciples have been invited to attend a wedding in Cana, and Mary is there too. John lets us in on a fascinating conversation. When the wine runs out, she says to Jesus, "They have no wine" (v. 3). Perhaps she is thinking both of the guests and of sparing the hosts of embarrassment.

Jesus seems to dismiss her concern: "Woman, what concern is that to you and to me? My hour has not yet come" (v. 4). Or perhaps, as the second sentence in his reply hints, he simply does not yet want to raise awareness of his messianic identity by performing a public miracle.

Jesus's address to his mother may seem striking to us. After all, in our culture, what loving son would call his mother "Woman"? It might seem cheeky, rude, or disrespectful, but it's not. The term John uses doesn't translate very well into modern English; it's not as formal as saying "yes, ma'am," but neither is it cold and impersonal. That's why, in some modern paraphrased versions of the Bible, such as *The Message*, Jesus just calls his mother "Mother."

But with John, words and events typically have both literal and symbolic meaning. There's a reason why Jesus addresses his mother as he does, and John wants us to stop and consider it. To gain a better understanding of why Jesus calls his mother "Woman," both at the wedding of Cana and at the cross, we need to go back to the magisterial and poetic beginning of John's Gospel—which very intentionally takes us all the way back to the opening verses of the Bible that describe how God spoke the world into existence:

> *In the beginning was the Word, and the Word was with God, and the Word was God. . . . All things came into being through him, and without him not one thing came into being. What has come into being in him was life, and the life was the light of all people.*
>
> *John 1:1, 3-4*

You may remember that Genesis begins in this way: "In the beginning when God created the heavens and the earth" (Genesis 1:1). The Creation story, of course, includes the creation of Adam and Eve, the first couple God joins together (2:18-24). Though there is no official wedding ceremony, God lovingly creates each of them for the other to become *one flesh*. In Genesis 1, God says, "Let us make humankind in our image" (1:26) and then proceeds to create male and female, leaving us to infer that both Adam and Eve were created at the same time. (In the perhaps more familiar Creation story in Genesis 2, which differs significantly in details and sequence from the story in Genesis 1, the man is fashioned from the "dust of the ground" [*adamah* in Hebrew], and the woman from the rib of the man [2:7, 21-22].) When the Creator of heaven and earth presents the bride to her groom, the groom's grateful response almost sounds breathless: "*This at last is bone of my bones / and flesh of my flesh; / this one shall be called Woman* [ishah in Hebrew], */ for out of Man* [ish] *this one was taken*" (2:23, emphasis added). The world's first couple was created in differentiated oneness in the image of the One who fashioned them. The woman is named Eve (*to give life* in Hebrew). Of course, it doesn't take long for the breathless gratitude to wane and for Adam and Eve to be tempted away from putting their full trust in God and to eat of the forbidden fruit (3:1-13) that God had instructed them to avoid. Adam and Eve devolve into blaming, finger-pointing, and hiding from God, and sin enters the world through them. But this doesn't change the reality that Eve is the "mother of all living" (3:20).

For John, the wedding at Cana calls to mind the first married couple in creation. Jesus has come to inaugurate a new creation and restore all that was destroyed in the original Paradise. The idea wasn't novel to John; decades earlier, in his First Letter to the Corinthians, Paul presents Jesus as the second Adam (1 Corinthians 15:45). The first man, Paul says, was from dust; the second man is from heaven. Jesus, the mind and spirit of God (the Word) made flesh in human form, will recapitulate what Adam did wrong, only to get it right this time. On the cross, he will rescue us from the sin and death that the first man brought into the world. And Jesus's mother? Just as Eve, the mother of all living, played a significant role in bringing about what is known as "the fall" of humanity, Jesus's mother, the one he calls "Woman," will play a significant role in its redemption. She gives birth and life to Jesus, the one who saves us. It is she who propels Jesus into his public ministry.

At the wedding at Cana, while the hour for Jesus's ministry to begin may not have come yet, his mother is nothing if not persistent. In response to Jesus's comment to her, "Woman,...My hour has not yet come" (John 2:4), she offers instructions to the wine stewards, reflecting her complete confidence that Jesus will act to repay the hospitality offered him by his hosts.[2] "Do whatever he tells you" (2:5), she says. His mother represents the model disciple who trusts in the saving action of her son. The nervous groom and thirsty guests, who are wondering about what happened to the wine, are about to experience a sign of the coming abundance Jesus will offer to the world as he performs his first miracle in an intimate setting among family and friends. After Jesus instructs the servants to fill large jars with water, they comply. But when the steward ladles out the liquid, it has turned into wine. And not just any wine: The wine that Jesus makes is the best at the celebration—so much so that the puzzled wine steward asks the bridegroom why they went against the custom of saving the cheaper wine to serve after the guests were drunk and wouldn't notice. Here again, John mixes literal details with symbolism.

An abundance of fine wine that Jesus produces from water segues his ministry into an abundance of bread for the hungry (6:5-14), an abundance of healing (4:46-54; 5:1-15; 9:1-7), an abundant catch of fish (21:1-14)—all symbolic of the abundant life Jesus came to offer the world ("I came that they might have life, and have it abundantly" [10:10b]). In his encounter with the Samaritan woman at the well (4:1-15), he offers not just ordinary water drawn from a bucket but a spring of living water that will never leave her thirsty again. This is part of what God in and through Jesus Christ imagines for our lives—a life filled with an abundance of peace and joy; a redeemed world where hunger and disease, and the systems that create them and lead to death, are swallowed up forever.

Jesus's mother, the model disciple, not only reminds us of the Creation story and the abundant life Jesus came to offer. Since in John's Gospel she appears only at the wedding in Cana and at the cross, she may also represent the scope of Jesus's incarnational ministry from its inception through its redemptive culmination.

At the cross, the scene is poignant. A lone male disciple, again described only in terms of his relationship to Jesus, accompanies this group of devoted and grieving women, remaining close not only to Jesus, but also to Jesus's mother. "The disciple whom he loved" (19:26), probably Jesus's best friend, stands beside Jesus's mother. Now that the hour of his death and glorification has come, Jesus offers the two people he loves most in the world some tender last words—words we are meant to overhear. When Jesus sees the two of them standing side by side at the cross, his heart is filled with compassion for his mother's grief and welfare, and he tenderly says to her, "Woman, here is your son." And to the disciple he says, "Here is your mother." Scripture goes on to tell us, "And from that hour the disciple took her into his own home" (19:26-27). Jesus's dying words are similar to those we hear from so many who yearn to impart their dying wishes to those they love—to their families—before their death: "Take care of each other." While they are similar on one level, on another they offer a yet deeper meaning.

The One Whom Jesus Loves

The disciple whom Jesus loves, like Jesus's mother, is never called by name in the Gospel of John. Each is referred to only according to their relationship to Jesus. The Beloved Disciple, as he has come to be known, is not introduced in John's Gospel until the night before Jesus's death. While Jesus and his disciples are eating dinner, the Beloved Disciple is described as reclining next to, or near, Jesus (John 13:23). He is present as Jesus gives his disciples a new commandment, "Just as I have loved you, you also should love one another" (13:34b). He is also a witness to the empty tomb (20:1-10) and is named as the disciple who recognizes the resurrected Christ in his appearance to his disciples at the Sea of Tiberias (21:7). While the Beloved Disciple is described as present at these particular events, no doubt he was also present with Jesus throughout his ministry as a witness to the abundance Jesus always brought out of scarcity. Thus, because he stays near Jesus at his death and at the tomb, and he recognizes Jesus through the abundant catch of fish that Jesus provides at the Sea of Tiberias, the Beloved Disciple, like Jesus's mother, is also a model disciple. That disciple is called to continue Jesus's ministry into the future.

I believe that the reason Jesus's mother and the Beloved Disciple are not named in this Gospel is so we can each identify ourselves as having the same intimate relationship with Jesus and character traits they had. We are meant to be the disciples who stay close to Jesus, who are near to hear his last words and instructions to us, who have confidence in and trust Jesus's provision of abundance in the midst of scarcity and hope in the midst of our own darkness. We are meant to experience the depth of his divine love and his desire to serve others out of that love. We are to experience the oneness with Jesus and the Father that has been intended since dawn of creation.

A NEW FAMILY

Nearness to and trust and confidence in Jesus also bring a new kind of kinship. In the prologue to his Gospel, John tells us, "But to all who received [Jesus], who believed in his name, he gave power to become children of God, who were born, not of blood...but *of* God" (John 1:12-13, emphasis added). You may have noticed that John's Gospel, unlike Matthew's and Luke's, dispenses with the details of Jesus's birth. And yet we often read John's prologue at Christmastime because John tells us what it all means. John doesn't bother with the "how"; John gives us the "why." In a bold, second act of creation, the Mind and Spirit of God came into the world as a human being: "The Word became flesh and lived among us" (1:14). And in making God's dwelling among us, the Creator of heaven and earth gave us the power to be born in a new way, not only as human children made in God's image, but as something much richer and deeper: children OF God. The Word made flesh gave us the power, as French theologian Pierre Teilhard de Chardin is credited with beautifully describing it, to move from human beings having a spiritual experience to spiritual beings having a human experience.[3] And in so doing, Jesus invited us into a family not bound by traditional lines of kinship or tribe, race, gender, or nationality.

Throughout his ministry, Jesus spoke of this new way of being. Luke's Gospel shares an episode when Jesus's mother and brothers show up while he is teaching in a synagogue. They can't get inside because of the large crowd, so someone passes the word to Jesus: "Your mother and your brothers are standing outside, wanting to see you." Instead of stopping like a dutiful son and asking the crowd to wait while he goes to his mother, Jesus replies with a statement that might seem shocking: "My mother and my brothers are those who hear the word of God and do it" (Luke 8:19-21). But Jesus is not attempting to be rude, nor divorcing himself from his family; he is extending the definition of what it means to be family. All of those who do God's will can be full members of this family.

After his resurrection, Jesus appears to his followers, who have become members of his family, but the Gospels do not mention him returning to his biological family. Luke's Gospel tells of Jesus's appearance to two of those followers, who are walking from Jerusalem to their home in Emmaus. Luke identifies only one of them: Cleopas. John identifies one of the women at the cross as the "wife of Clopas." Some scholars suggest that Clopas and Cleopas are the same person, and that Jesus appeared to a married couple who invited him into their home—as family.[4]

The New Testament Greek word that we translate as "church" is *ekklesia*. (In Spanish it becomes *iglesia*.) In Greek it means "the assembly." In the Greek translation of the Old Testament, *ekklesia* refers to a Hebrew word that means all of the people together. The assembly of ancient Israel consisted of twelve tribes. In choosing twelve disciples, Jesus is making a statement: he is redefining what it means to be part of the community, and he is expanding its boundaries far beyond the way the assembly had been understood previously. When he nicknames Peter "the rock" and tells him that on this rock I will build my *ekklesia*—my new community, he is referring to Peter's declaration of faith in Jesus as the Messiah. For Jesus, anyone who has faith in him can be part of this incredibly inclusive, far-reaching community. By doing the will of God, they place themselves under the kingship of Christ and enter into the Kingdom.

On the cross, Jesus again invokes this new community as a dying wish. When Jesus looks down at his grieving mother and the disciple and says, "'Woman, here is your son.'... 'Here is your mother,'" he is doing more than ensuring his mother is cared for after his death. The relationship that Jesus's mother and the disciple whom he loved share with Jesus, the same relationship we can share with Jesus, creates a new kind of family.

Many scholars assume that Jesus's mother is a widow at the time of his death, since the last time Joseph is mentioned in any of the Gospels is in the story of Jesus's visit to the Temple as a twelve-year-old (Luke 2:41-51). Jesus's brothers would have assumed the responsibility of caring for their mother's welfare upon the death of her oldest son. Leaving his mother in the care of the Beloved Disciple is an act of creation—as Jesus creates and defines a new family of faith. While the defining moment in the birth of the church in the Book of Acts is described in the dramatic coming of the Holy Spirit on the believers at Pentecost (Acts 2), in John's Gospel the creation of the church begins at the cross. Jesus, through the words he speaks to his mother and friend, creates the church, and that church becomes family to one another! Jesus's mother and the Beloved Disciple are not blood relatives, but they have developed a spiritual kinship through their trust in Jesus and his heavenly Father, a kinship that is cemented in the hour of Jesus's death.

In the moment that he leaves his mother and the Beloved Disciple in the care of one another, Jesus left all who would be future followers—he left *us*, his family—in the care of one another as well. As the family of Christ, we are called to heed Christ's final instructions and follow the example of those gathered near the cross. We are the extension of Christ's love and care for God's children.

This call into a new community was always part of the understanding of the early followers of Jesus. It is why, in the Christian assemblies that Paul nurtured in modern-day Turkey and Greece, the apostle insisted that, within the body of Christ, there must be no distinctions between Jews and Gentiles, slaves and free persons, men and women. Sure, the larger, secular world still arranged itself around those categories—Roman society was built upon the pillars of slavery and patriarchy—but Christians were part of a new community in which such human distinctions were inoperative and must be set aside in the way they related to each other. It is why Paul insisted that Christians should focus on building each other up so that we become "rooted and grounded in love" (Ephesians 3:17). It is why he insisted that the Corinthians, who separated themselves by wealth and social class in the Greco-Roman fashion, were observing what was supposed to be a common meal in an unworthy way (1 Corinthians 11:17-22); in essence, Paul was saying, "We are all family in Christ, and you don't treat family like that."

Most of us, I suspect, know people in our church or community who have been family to us or to our children. In my own life, our family of faith has been as close as family to us. When our children were born, or when there was a death in our biological family, we would find meals delivered to our front porch; our mailbox would overflow with notes of congratulations or condolence. We would be flooded with phone calls asking what kind of help we needed or offering a sympathetic ear. When our children married, members of our Sunday school class offered to host engagement showers, and it was these same people our children insisted we invite to their weddings because those were the people who had most surrounded them in love and had provided the greatest example of Christ to them as they grew up.

I hear often from people for whom the church has been like family. More than one has said that it was the church staff or members of a small group or Sunday morning class who visited them in the hospital, who wrote letters to them in prison, who found a way to help them through financial struggles, who helped them find a job, who sat with them through the years of darkness of losing a child. That is the kind of new community that Christ proclaimed (it's worth remembering here that, in English, *community*, *common*, and *communion* all come from the same root). That is the kind of new family that Jesus called into being with his words from the cross.

WAYS OF BEING FAMILY

During this past year, as biological families have been isolated and travel has been difficult, friends and neighbors have become grandparents, mothers, fathers, and children to each other. I suspect that many of you have fulfilled that role for others. Perhaps you delivered meals and prescriptions to those in need. Or you volunteered to make phone calls to see if there were any unmet needs among "family." As of this writing, the catering kitchen at our church has produced more than 220,000 box lunches to feed those in need in the community, including schoolchildren whose primary source of nutrition comes from breakfast and lunch provided at their school.

Early in the pandemic, during one of our church all-staff video conferences, our senior minister said what many of you probably heard as well: "Please don't say the church is closed! The church building may be closed, but the church is not closed. Friends, YOU are the church. WE, as the body of Christ, are the church, and *we* are not closed." I don't know what will be officially open and what will remain closed by the date of this book's publication, but I do know that something in your life and in the world will feel closed off to you. Today, you may be experiencing a Good Friday, a day of suffering, grieving, and apparent defeat. You may have places in your life that feel closed off, some obstacles in your life to get around. We are all guaranteed to have to find new ways of doing old things. Today may seem like Good Friday to some economically, physically, or spiritually, but the hope of the Resurrection is ever among us. We may have to find new ways to do or access old things, but our mission is the same as it has been for 2,000 years: to love one another as Christ loved us and to extend the idea of neighbor, community, and family to the people whom God places in our path, whoever and wherever they are. The new family goes far beyond our Christian assemblies. As Jesus taught, whenever we encounter those who are hungry or need clothing, or who are ill or in prison, we encounter Jesus; whatever we do, or fail to do, for "the least of these" in God's family, that is what we do, or fail to do, for Jesus (from Matthew 25:35-43).

The novel coronavirus, for all of the bad that has happened, has not only forced us to find new ways to do old things but has also called us to take stock of what is really important in life. I've never seen more families, more moms and dads and children and grandparents, out walking and riding bikes as I have during these past few months. There have been more phone calls and FaceTime with friends and family. More people we know have vowed to refrain from using vitriolic or divisive statements on their social media pages. We're trying our best to support our local businesses from afar. But more importantly, this time has given me, and I hope this season gives you, time to lean in and listen to Jesus. Time to stand near his cross and really hear his words. Time to cling to the one who is unchanging in uncertain times. Just as you have been especially careful about taking care of yourself physically over the past year, I hope you are caring for yourself spiritually as well. We have all washed our hands thousands of times over the past several months. I hope during this season that you can discern what things in your life should remain the same, what elements just need a small touch-up, and what, if anything, Jesus would like for you to allow him to completely rework. As you wait for Easter and Resurrection, ask yourself, "Where do I need more abundance, more newness of life? What or who in my sphere of influence needs more abundance or newness of life? How is Jesus calling me to be family to someone else? Who is the mother Jesus is asking me to care for who is not my biological mother? Whom should I look after like a son or daughter? Who needs me to be family to them? And how will living into Jesus's words to the Beloved Disciple bring me into a new way of being—a resurrection?

Death did not have the last word in Jesus's life. The coronavirus, the stock market, the political climate, or whatever the crisis *du jour* may be: these will not have the last word on our lives either. Through the power of the Resurrection, God can take that which appears demolished and impassible and turn it into a beautiful new way forward.

On the other side of Good Friday, things were never the same for Jesus's followers. Jesus's resurrection brought abundant life to them they could have never imagined. Although they continued to face challenges and obstacles to overcome, they became a new creation, a new church, a massive new family that grew from a tiny cohort in Jerusalem to reach every part of the vast Roman Empire. Whatever Good Fridays we face, we will never be the same either. Through the power of the resurrected Christ, we can be something new, something transformed. Jesus can take what seems a demolished mess and turn it into something beautiful. Let that be our hope because that is his promise. Lean in. Listen. Be family to one another.

I Am
Thirsty

Chapter 5

I AM THIRSTY

After this, when Jesus knew that all was now finished,
he said (in order to fulfill the scripture), "I am thirsty." A
jar full of sour wine was standing there. So they put a
sponge full of the wine on a branch of hyssop and held
it to his mouth.

John 19:28-29

Two years ago, my heart sank when I saw my sister-in-law's name pop up on the screen of my ringing cellphone. My brother had been battling cancer for several years but recently had been doing quite well. However, since my husband and I were out of town, I sensed my sister-in-law had not initiated this call to conduct a friendly chat. I answered the phone to hear her quavering voice, "Mike has been admitted to MD Anderson Cancer Center in Houston and is not doing well. It doesn't look good." During the drive from Dallas to Houston to be with Mike and his family, I kept hoping to make it in time to hear his voice one more time and to tell him how much I loved him. I was also flooded with memories of our life together.

Perhaps our bond was so close because we lived in a rural area, and often we were the only playmates the other had. I was five years younger than Mike, and he was desperate to play sports. So, he taught me how to wrestle; how to pitch, bat, and catch a baseball; how to shoot a BB gun; and how to throw a football with a tight spiral. At times I even served as his tackling dummy. Always gentle, Mike would get on his knees to "run" against five-year-old me to practice his tackling skills. Reciprocally, Mike was just as willing to be a playmate for me. He was a patient tea party participant, doll rocker, blanket fort maker, and ballet partner. We taught each other well, and we adored each other. In our family, family was everything. So, as we grew up, married, and had children, the other's family became as dear to us as we were to each other.

Mike's personality was effervescent. His laughter, life, and love came bubbling up and pouring out to all who would come near and catch what was spilling over. Now, as we drove to Houston, I longed for, thirsted for, one more moment of my brother, his big laugh, and his protective arm around my shoulder. My hopes were dashed when I arrived at the hospital to discover that my brother had become mostly unresponsive and uncommunicative. "That's okay," I thought. "There really wasn't anything left unsaid in our relationship." There wasn't a time when our families were together that we didn't part without saying, "I love you." So, we gathered around his bed as a family, told stories about his life, laughed as we retold his old jokes, and cried and hugged each other so tightly we could hardly breathe. Occasionally, with closed eyes, he would smile faintly as if to acknowledge that he heard us and was actually part of the conversation, even if he was unable to speak.

One afternoon, I offered to stay at his bedside while others stepped out for lunch. As I leaned over his bed, telling Mike how much I loved him, something surprising happened. His eyes flew open wide, and I felt the grip of his strong hand around the back of my neck pulling my face close to his. Then he kissed me on the cheek and said very clearly, "I love you." Those were the last words I heard him speak before his death. There was yet a sip of life and love left to be shared, and it was sweet. "I love you." What a gift those words are to hear, to speak, and to experience.

To know we are loved and valued: Isn't that what all of us are most thirsty for in life? We know that children who receive no words or love, no physical touch, and little to no human interaction as infants are unable to develop and thrive cognitively, physically, and emotionally. To know love, to be loved, and to love others is our greatest need and purpose in life. That was the heart of Jesus's ministry (John 13:34).

Jesus's actions on the cross conveyed the deep love he had for the world. He lived out in death the deep love of God that he shared with people in life. Wherever he went, crowds gathered from miles away to catch as much as they could of the warmth, love, faith, teaching, and healing that bubbled up and out from him. While many people imagine and preach Jesus as mostly a man of sorrows, very serious, and judgmental, I imagine him as mostly joyful, smiling, effervescent as he worked diligently to transform the sorrows of this world through his loving actions. Except on Good Friday. Although Jesus will come into his glory on this day, in John's Gospel, after he takes care of the needs of his mother and makes provision for the future of his church, Jesus's suffering humanity is also on full display.

Sometimes it's easy to forget, as we imagine the full divinity of Jesus—in his changing water into wine; feeding large crowds of people; healing countless sick, lame, and blind people; and raising the dead—that he was also fully human. Really and truly human. Matthew and Mark clearly make this point in the words they record Jesus speaking from the cross, "My God, my God, why have you forsaken me?" The writer of John's Gospel wants us to take note of Jesus's humanity at the cross as well. In fact, it is all the more powerfully resonant because John, above all the other Gospels, emphasizes Jesus's divinity as the Word who was God and was with God in the beginning.

Ever true to the multifaceted nature of the Fourth Gospel, Jesus's words, "I am thirsty," have both literal and symbolic meaning. They also carry with them deep theological significance. Why should we lean in to hear this short, simple sentence? What relevance to our lives and our journey with Jesus could "I am thirsty" possibly hold? That's what we're about to explore.

FULLY HUMAN

While all four Gospels tell us that Jesus was offered sour wine to drink from a sponge as he was dying on the cross, only the Gospel of John records these words from Jesus, "I am thirsty." John tells us that Jesus said these words to fulfill scripture. The scripture to which John's Gospel alludes is Psalm 69:21: "They gave me poison for food, / and for my thirst they gave me vinegar to drink." Matthew and Mark record that Jesus is *offered* wine mixed with myrrh or gall, but that he refuses to drink it (Mark 15:22-23; Matthew 27:34). Some suggest that the myrrh or gall added to the wine might have acted as an anesthetic or poison to help relieve Jesus's pain or hasten his death.[1] Jesus refuses to be anesthetized as he drinks from the figurative cup from which he previously asked to be delivered. Jesus faces his death and the sinfulness of humanity with eyes wide open and fully awake. He says these words to fulfill scripture, but Jesus is also in pain—and as the scorching Judean sun beats down on his head in the heat of the afternoon, Jesus is thirsty. Thirst is a common feeling among people who are dying of injuries and loss of blood. In expressing his thirst, Jesus is experiencing a physical death on human terms. He is showing that he is with us and one of us.

Even today, many people think that while Jesus may be both divine and human, his divinity somehow made him a little *less* human, that he didn't suffer as much as you or I might as human beings. Other people, both today and in John's day, believed that Jesus only appeared to be suffering on the cross, that he only *seemed* to be human. God would never allow God's own self to suffer, right? This belief is called Docetism, from the Greek word *dokein*, meaning "to seem." Yet the Gospels are clear that, while Jesus stilled storms and raised the dead, he was also hungry and sleepy; felt pain, joy, and love; and experienced thirst just as you and I. Thus, one reason John's Gospel records Jesus saying "I am thirsty" from the cross is to make certain we know that Jesus understands everything we are experiencing physically. When you are hungry, thirsty, or heartbroken—whether you have a small touch of stomach flu or stage four cancer, when you are your most joyful or in your deepest grief—Jesus fully understands you because he is fully human. In life and in death on the cross, he underwent the full range of emotions and physical sensory experiences that you do. All of them. So as you bear your own crosses in life, know that when you lift your heart and voice to Jesus, not only are you praying to the Divine One who is all-knowing, you are also praying to the human Jesus who understands everything you are encountering because he has experienced it before you, and because you are his child, he experiences it with you. You are not alone.

SPIRITUAL THIRST

At my childhood home in the country, we had the good fortune of having a large pond on our property—our very own swimming hole. We added a makeshift diving board and a rope swing that would deliver us out into the pond's deep, cool waters. What I noticed about this pond was that the water never warmed up in the summer. It was always cool and refreshing, no matter how high the temperatures in July and August soared. So, one day I asked my dad, "Why does this water never get warm like the local swimming pool in the summer?" He said, "That's because it's spring-fed."

Pointing to a weeping willow tree that grew near the banks of the pond, he continued, "There is an underground spring that bubbles up right over there, and we have a pipe that allows some of that water to flow into the pond. We walked over, and he showed me. Right beside the weeping willow that shaded one side of the pond was a pipe, and out of it flowed clear, cold water. Dad said the water was probably safe for drinking, as it fed our local water supply, quenching an entire community's thirst. Not only did the water in our pond never get warm, it never failed to replenish itself. We didn't have to worry about rainfall to keep it full, and there was a constant source of fresh, clear, flowing water for us to swim and fish in.

The word *spirit* in Greek is *pneuma*, which can also mean *wind* or *breath*. John's Gospel consistently draws attention to the work of God's Spirit. On Jesus's last night with his disciples, he tells them that, while he can no longer remain with them, the Spirit (or Advocate) will come abide with them forever (John 14:16). When he appears to them after his resurrection, he breathes on them and says, "Receive the Holy Spirit" (20:22). And because John has begun his Gospel with a reference to what happens "in the beginning," he wants us to make the connection to the Creation story, when God breathed life into Adam; now, God through Jesus is breathing a new kind of life into his followers.

But elsewhere in the Gospel of John, the writer describes the coming of the Holy Spirit in a less dramatic but no less important way. In two places, Jesus speaks of the Holy Spirit, his Spirit, as thirst-quenching, as a spring of living water that will never run dry and that bubbles up to abundant and eternal life (7:37-39; 4:10, 13-14).

When Jesus first uses this metaphor to describe himself, it is at a water well in Samaria, near the village of Sychar (4:5-6). While his disciples go into town to buy food, Jesus remains behind, and he meets a Samaritan woman who has come to draw water. Unlike other women, who tended to come as a group early in the morning, this woman waits until the middle of the day, when she expects no one else to be around—a detail that offers a clue as to her status and reputation in the community. During their conversation, Jesus offers her the promise of "living water" that will never leave her thirsty again (4:10, 13-14). She jumps at the opportunity and runs to tell her neighbors that she has met the promised Messiah (Samaritans, descended from Jews of the Northern Kingdom of Israel, also looked forward to the coming of the Messiah)—and through her witness, John says, many in her community came to believe in Jesus (4:28-29, 39).

Later, Jesus is in Jerusalem for the festival of Tabernacles (also known as the Feast of Booths or Sukkot), which commemorates the wanderings of the children of Israel in the wilderness. Originally a harvest festival, it came to be associated with the eschatological hope for a time when God's life-giving presence would flow out in rivers from the Temple (Ezekiel 47:12), like water from the rock in the wilderness (Exodus 17:1-7). As part of the festival, the priest would pour fresh water on the altar as an offering to God, a remembrance of how God provided water for the Israelites in the desert. At this point, according to John, Jesus cries out: "Let anyone who is thirsty come to me, and let the one who believes in me drink." Then he paraphrases a scripture: "'Out of the believer's heart shall flow rivers of living water'" (John 7:37-39).

Jesus's words would have reminded the readers of John's Gospel of God's call to Israel through the prophet Isaiah:

> *Ho, everyone who thirsts,*
> *come to the waters;*

and you that have no money,
    come, buy and eat!
Come, buy wine and milk
    without money and without price.
Why do you spend your money for that which is
not bread,
        and your labor for that which does not satisfy?
                                    Isaiah 55:1-2a

WHAT ARE WE THIRSTY FOR?

God is offering Israel this abundant life. Jesus, the Word made flesh, has come to do the same. The breath and Spirit of God are active in the Old Testament and the New. People in Jesus's day—as in Old Testament days and our own day—are thirsty. They thirst for justice and righteousness to flow down like rivers. They are thirsty for a messiah. They are thirsty for freedom from oppression. They are thirsty to be valued. They are thirsty for that which the leaders and politicians have not been able to satisfy.

Advertising companies know we are thirsty and have learned to talk like the prophets and Jesus. "Let anyone who thirsts, come over here," their messages promise in one form or another. "If you love her, this diamond will prove it....Happiness can be found in this car, this diet plan, this dress, this vacation, this cosmetic cream or procedure." Even what we would otherwise call junk food—a candy bar—is presented as what we need to satisfy our hunger so we can be ourselves again. We are thirsty to be adored, thin, powerful, exciting, and young. But we are likely to find that none of these attributes or material things can truly satisfy us. In fact, they can leave us even worse off than before because they are fundamentally unsatisfying.

Why waste your time, says Isaiah, on things that do not satisfy—especially when you can have the living water of love, joy, peace, and justice? That is what Jesus offers the woman at the well and the people at the festival. He speaks clearly to us, as people who have drunk from the well of our culture and found that it gives us only empty calories. We eat and drink and soon are hungry and thirsty again for more. Jesus calls to people who want more. John Wesley called this kind of quenching, this kind of work of the Holy Spirit, sanctification—being perfected in love as Christ's Spirit works within us, transforming us, and as we become more and more like Christ. The Holy Spirit's work is to make us thirsty for what God wants in the world and to offer us the abundant life that only life in relationship with God through Jesus Christ can satisfy: a life of love of God and neighbor.

Jesus said, "Out of the believer's heart shall flow rivers of living water" (John 7:38). Jesus is the source of that living water, that abundant life, but it will flow from believers as well. To believe in Jesus is to trust him and to follow in his way, to do what he did. He shared everything he had from his Father. He loved others. He fed the hungry, healed the sick, and ate with outcasts and sinners. Those who trust Jesus are called to do the same, to love one another "as I have loved you" (13:34). That love pours from his heart to ours and out to a thirsty world.

The Greek word for "heart" in this verse is *koilia*. It can also mean "womb" or "belly," which carries with it a connotation of bringing new life. Nicodemus, who comes at night asking questions of Jesus in John's Gospel, is told he must be born again. By way of reply, he asks, Can a person enter into the koilia, the womb, a second time? (3:4, paraphrased). No, we are born by water (natural birth) and the Spirit. When we place our faith in Jesus, his Spirit gives us the power to live as he lived. The thirst in our souls is quenched, and we experience new life, as do those around us.

A JAR OF SOUR WINE

At Jesus's cry, "I am thirsty," scripture notes: "A jar full of sour wine was standing there. So they put a sponge full of the wine on a branch of hyssop and held it to his mouth" (John 19:29). A jar full of sour wine certainly didn't compare to the jars full of fine, abundant wine that Jesus provided for the host of the wedding party at the beginning of his ministry. The wine he offers is sweet. The wine offered to him, the cup he drinks in death, is sour.

And yet, John's Gospel shows us that Jesus is confident and in control of the matters surrounding his death. At an earlier point in his ministry, he says: "I am the good shepherd. The good shepherd lays down his life for the sheep. . . . I lay down my life in order to take it up again. No one takes it from me, but I lay it down of my own accord. I have power to lay it down, and I have power to take it up again" (10:11, 17b-18a). He reinforces that message at the time of his arrest. When Peter intervenes to try to save Jesus, he rebukes him: "Am I not to drink the cup that the Father has given me?" (18:11).

Other Gospels record that Jesus refuses the wine offered him on the cross. John's Gospel is the only one to observe that Jesus receives this wine, and it is offered to him from a hyssop branch. Hyssop is a brushy bush. Some argue that a hyssop branch probably couldn't support a sponge, while others say there are varieties of hyssop, and that its leaves and branches would be relatively absorptive. In any event, the author of John is often concerned as much with symbolic meanings as with particular details.

And the symbolism here is powerful. John tells us that Jesus was sent to his death at noon on the day of Preparation for the Passover—the day and the time the Passover lambs are slaughtered (19:14-16).[2] It may not be obvious to modern-day Christians, but readers of John's Gospel would have immediately made the connection between the hyssop branch that delivers the sour red wine to Jesus's lips and his crucifixion on the day of Preparation for the Passover. For Christians, God's mightiest act of salvation occurred in the death and resurrection of Jesus, and we commemorate that act with joyous celebration each Easter. For Jews in Jesus's day, and for Jesus and his family, God's mightiest act of salvation was Passover, which commemorates God's rescue of God's people from slavery in Egypt. On the final night of their captivity, God sends the last of ten plagues to secure their deliverance from bondage to Pharaoh. Death was to strike every firstborn in the land of Egypt, humans and animals alike. To save the Israelites from this disastrous plague, God instructs Moses to tell them to select lambs without blemish and slaughter them. Before they cooked the lambs to eat with their families, they were to dip a branch of *hyssop* into the blood of the lamb, mark the doorposts of their homes with it, and stay inside. As death made its way through the streets of Egypt, it *passed over* those homes marked with the blood of the lambs, and the Israelites were saved (Exodus 12). Pharaoh released the Israelites from their bondage, and they were free (at least until Pharaoh hardened his heart and sent his chariots to stop the people at the sea, leading to another mighty act of deliverance) to follow God's lead into the Promised Land—into a better life and brighter future. Hyssop is also mentioned in the Book of Hebrews, describing Moses sprinkling the scroll of the law and all of the people with blood saying, "This is the blood of the covenant that God has ordained for you" (Hebrews 9:19-20; refer to Exodus 24:8).

John's connection of the hyssop to Jesus's crucifixion on the day of Preparation is intentional. It sends a clear message that Jesus is our Passover Lamb who saves us from death and delivers us from slavery—not the type of physical bondage that the people experienced in Egypt but from slavery to sin that leads to death. While Passover lambs were not sacrificed for the forgiveness of sins, but to celebrate deliverance from death and slavery, Jesus says of the cup he lifts at his last Passover meal, "This is my blood of the covenant, which is poured out for many" (Mark 14:24). Matthew's Gospel expands Jesus's words to include that his blood is "poured out for many for the forgiveness of sins" (26:28). Luke describes Jesus's cup at Passover in this way: "This cup that is poured out for you is the new covenant in my blood" (22:20b).

Those who gather at the cross on Good Friday hear Jesus's words of physical pain, "I am thirsty." Someone, perhaps one of his dear friends standing with him, acts to relieve his discomfort, just as many of us have offered a drink to someone we knew who was dying. Those who have ears to hear also know that Jesus is spiritually thirsty because he has drunk the bitter cup of death, and the one who offers living water bubbling up to eternal life is parched, bone-dry. It has all been poured out for them—and for you.

In his letter to the believers at Philippi, a Christian community that he dearly loved, the apostle Paul uses this same metaphor of self-emptying, pouring out, to describe what Jesus did for us on the cross—and what his followers are called to do for others through acts of self-giving love. "Do nothing from selfish ambition or conceit," he urges them, "but in humility regard others as better than yourselves. Let each of you look not to your own interests, but to the interests of others. Let the same mind be in you that was in Christ Jesus" (Philippians 2:3-5).

And what was the mindset of Jesus that we should emulate? Paul proceeds to quote what apparently was an early Christian hymn:

> *Though he was in the form of God,*
> *[he] did not regard equality with God*
> *as something to be exploited,*
> *but emptied himself,*
> *taking the form of a slave,*
> *being born in human likeness.*

And being found in human form,
he humbled himself
and became obedient to the point of death—
even death on a cross.

Therefore God also highly exalted him
and gave him the name
that is above every name,
so that at the name of Jesus
every knee should bend,
in heaven and on earth and under the earth,
and every tongue should confess
that Jesus Christ is Lord,
to the glory of God the Father.

Philippians 2:6-11

BEING LIVING WATER

Through his own Spirit, poured out for us and into us, we can relieve his thirst as we serve those who suffer: "'I was thirsty and you gave me something to drink.' ... 'Just as you did it to one of the least of these who are members of my family, you did it to me'" (Matthew 25:35b, 40b). When we drink deeply from the living water that Jesus offers, it not only satisfies us. It transforms and empowers us to be for others what Jesus is for us.

We all thirst for a less vitriolic and more peaceful nation and world. We hope that we all become kinder, gentler, more patient, more like Jesus. We all hope that the pace of the world slows a bit, becomes less frantic.

As you have been engaging in this journey to the cross during Lent, I wonder what the Holy Spirit has been stirring in your heart. What flames have emerged? What thirsts have you felt, and what thirsts have been quenched?

Perhaps even more to the point of Jesus's last words, where are you being called to give of yourself? Where is Jesus calling you to take the form of a servant? Where is Jesus inviting you to share his mindset and pour yourself out on behalf of those who are thirsting for love, for hope, for physical needs to be addressed, for bonds of oppression to be broken, or simply to be treated as if their lives matter?

Maybe you are ready to pour yourself out to help feed the hungry, or literally quench the thirst of those who don't have clean drinking water. Maybe you're ready to satisfy someone's thirst for literacy, to help underserved children in your city improve their reading scores. Perhaps a gentle wind is pushing you to reach out and help those who are experiencing domestic violence. Is the Spirit moving you to pick up the phone and make a call to restore a relationship? Are you feeling the rush of a wind to quench the thirst of those who are experiencing injustice?

This past year, within a two-week period we saw images on television of God's breath being squeezed out of George Floyd, of Ahmaud Arbery being shot jogging through a neighborhood, and of a white woman putting the life of an African American bird-watcher at risk in New York's Central Park by calling the police and falsely claiming that he was threatening her. No doubt, this innocent man was afraid that what had happened to Floyd and Arbery and so many others might happen to him. Those incidents made me think of a white friend and his African American wife who have adopted three young African American children. I have become painfully aware of how this couple must fear for their children growing up in a society where going out to play, to jog, to shop, just to watch birds in the park, or to walk in your own neighborhood with a hoodie pulled over your head is to be at risk. In a few years, these parents will have to worry about what might happen if their children are stopped for a minor traffic violation. They will have to have "the talk" that Black parents have with their sons and daughters about how to navigate their way carefully in a world where they have too often been viewed differently.

This couple, and millions of others like them, are thirsty. They are thirsty for the world to see them and their children as the precious children of God that they are. They are thirsty for justice to roll down like waters and righteousness like an ever-flowing stream (Amos 5:24). May we thirst with them and with all who find themselves longing to be loved and valued as God values them; may all of our actions offer cool water for their parched places; may we remember and live out what the Teacher taught us: "Blessed are those who hunger and thirst for righteousness, for they will be filled" (Matthew 5:6).

In pouring ourselves out for others who are thirsty, we find that our own thirst is relieved. We find that we are able to access the living water that will never leave us thirsty again, a stream that flows into eternal life. To borrow from the prayer commonly attributed to Francis of Assisi:[3]

> Lord, let us be instruments of your peace;
> where there is hatred, let us sow love;
> where there is injury, pardon;
> where there is doubt, faith;
> where there is despair, hope;
> where there is darkness, light;
> and where there is sadness, joy.
>
> O Divine Master,
> grant that I may not so much seek
> to be consoled as to console;
> to be understood, as to understand;

to be loved, as to love;
for it is in giving that we receive,
it is in pardoning that we are pardoned,
and it is in dying that we are born to eternal life.

Jesus's words "I am thirsty" are meant to be consumed, drunk in deeply, for they are filled with the sweetness of the meaning of his death. And part of that meaning is the promise of fulfillment and · triumph. As St. Francis recognized, it is in the giving of ourselves that we find the greatest gift of all. It is in pouring ourselves out on behalf of others that we find ourselves perpetually filled with the water that never leaves us thirsty again.

Drink deeply. The world is thirsty, and we've been offered an abundance of Living Water.

CHAPTER 6

Into Your Hands

Chapter 6

INTO YOUR HANDS

When Jesus had received the wine, he said, "It is finished." Then he bowed his head and gave up his spirit.
                                                          John 19:30

It was now about noon, and darkness came over the whole land until three in the afternoon, while the sun's light failed; and the curtain of the temple was torn in two. Then Jesus, crying with a loud voice, said, "Father, into your hands I commend my spirit." Having said this, he breathed his last.
                                                          Luke 23:44-46

THIN PLACES

Iona is an island off the west coast of Scotland. Exiled from his native Ireland, St. Columba came to Iona with twelve companions in AD 563 and established a monastery. But they didn't stop there. Irish monks from Iona brought Christianity to Scotland. Their influence was so strong that they gave the country its name. The Romans had called the place the land of the Pictii (Picts), or "picture people," for the tattoos that covered their bodies. With the coming of Celtic Christianity, the land came to be known as Scotland, derived from "Scotus," which means "Irish."

As early as the seventh century, Christian pilgrims were coming to Iona, and today they flock there still. When they see Iona for themselves and walk on the grounds of the abbey that stands on the site of Columba's original church, they understand why the Celts call it a "thin place." To them, a thin place is where heaven and earth seem to touch, where the veil between heaven and earth is negligible. George Macleod, founder of the current Iona Community, said that Iona is a "thin place where only tissue paper separates the material from the spiritual."[1] The sense is so strong that innumerable people who would describe themselves as non-religious have reported experiencing a spiritual awakening when they visit Iona.

However, Iona isn't unique. Thin places can be found most anywhere: at the beach, or in quiet corners of our homes while we pray or read the Bible. For me, the Rocky Mountains in Colorado are such a thin place that I might as well have been on a pilgrimage to Iona. When I visit there with my family, escaping the sweltering summer heat of Texas, we wake up every morning to refreshing fifty-degree temperatures in the summer, and we take long hikes in the mountains. As we explore the mountains, we marvel at the beauty of the aspens, the magnificent array of wildflowers, and the wildlife all around us. As I look up at the grandeur of mountain peaks during my morning devotional time, it is easy to sense God's presence so profoundly in that place. It is easy to feel close to God. (It's no wonder that Jesus, too, found the mountains to be a thin place where he would often go to pray.)

In the Old Testament, Jacob finds a thin place, too. Escaping the combustive heat of his home life (his brother, Esau, you may recall, has threatened to kill him for stealing their father's blessing, and their mother has urged him to seek the protection of his uncle in a foreign land), Jacob stops from his travels to rest for the night (Genesis 28:10-19). He's not in a beautiful mountain landscape but a rocky wilderness, and right there, in the middle of nowhere, he experiences a thin place. As he settles into a deep sleep with his cheek resting against the warmth of a desert rock-turned-pillow, he has a vivid dream. He sees a stairway set up on earth, with the top of it reaching to heaven and the angels of God ascending and descending on it like a celestial escalator. Then all of a sudden, God is right there beside Jacob, without any warning or fanfare, just as God had appeared to his grandfather Abraham. God renews with Jacob the covenant promises he made to Abraham: safety, land, and children—lots of children—and that he and his family will be a blessing to all of the families of the earth. When Jacob wakes up, he exclaims, God was in this place and I didn't even know it! He called this thin place "Bethel," which means House of God. Thin places can be found most anywhere. Even in the wilderness places and moments of our own lives.

I've said before that sometimes I have the holy privilege of being invited into the intimacy of families' lives as a loved one is dying. It's in those moments where families often experience a thin place where God seems most present in their final hours together. I know I feel it in those moments. The same was true for those present at Jesus's death as they overhear his last words, some directed to them, others meant for them to overhear, but symbolically a thin place erupts.

THE CURTAIN TORN

Luke's Gospel tells us that Jesus was crucified between two criminals, beginning at about nine o'clock in the morning. He has been awake all night following his arrest, interrogation, and appearance before the council of religious leaders, the Sanhedrin. He has endured the physical pain of a severe flogging, then was forced to carry a heavy crossbeam from inside the city to the place of execution. He has endured the emotional pain of being mocked, spat upon, and betrayed. And all of that has taken place before he is even nailed to the beam and lifted up onto the cross.

Jesus hangs on the cross for six long, excruciating hours (when we describe pain we feel as excruciating, we probably don't realize that the word originated from the pain of enduring a crucifixion). Those who witnessed Jesus's death might have felt like they were in the opposite of a thin place—somewhere that God seemed to be absent rather than overwhelmingly present. It seemed supernatural. Around noon, the whole sky turned dark, and Luke reports that the darkness covered "the whole land" for the hours before Jesus's death (Luke 23:44). It was as if the entire cosmos, or God's own self, was mourning the impending death of the Son of God. It is certainly Jesus's darkest hour and the darkest hour for those who love him and have followed him. Their dreams for a great future in Jesus's kingdom, their hopes that he was the Messiah, the one to save Israel, seemed to have been completely dashed. In the midst of the darkness, when all seems lost, just as Jesus breathes his last, Luke tells us that "the curtain of the temple [in Jerusalem] was torn in two" (23:45). Matthew and Mark echo this detail, although they record that the curtain is torn just after Jesus breathes his last. The inclusion of this event in three of the four Gospels is significant.

Within the Temple walls there was an inner court, designated only for priests, called the Holy Place. Within the Holy Place was the inner sanctuary, the Holy of Holies, a separate area that had contained the ark of the covenant. The ark was an ornate wooden box overlaid with gold that held the Ten Commandments, which were given to Moses by God on Mount Sinai. The wings of two golden cherubim seated on top of the ark created what was known as the Mercy Seat, considered to be God's own throne. God's very presence was said to dwell within the Holy of Holies. A thick curtain, or veil of covering, separated the Holy Place from the Holy of Holies. The ark disappeared around the time of the destruction of the Temple by the Babylonians in 587 BC (some suggest that escaping Jews carried it to safety in Egypt). But even after the exile in Babylon ended and a second Temple was built, the Holy of Holies (minus the original ark) remained. Only the high priest was allowed to enter the Holy of Holies, and even he could go inside only once a year, during the Day of Atonement, to offer sacrifices to atone for his sins and the sins of the people. There, he would sprinkle the blood of a sacrificed calf and goat for sins intentional and unintentional.

The tearing of the Temple curtain, the veil between the presence of God and the people of God, was one of many symbols for what Jesus's self-sacrificing death accomplished on the cross. There, Jesus became our high priest to offer us direct access to God's own presence, for forgiveness for our sins once and for all. His was the final and perfect sacrifice. Hebrews 9:11-12 explains it this way: "But when Christ came as a high priest... he entered once for all into the Holy Place, not with the blood of goats and calves, but with his own blood, thus obtaining eternal redemption."

Through Jesus's laying down of his life for his sheep, for all of humanity, God and humanity are reconciled, and all the earth becomes a thin place through Jesus Christ. There is no veil, no curtain, separating us from the love and mercy of God in Christ Jesus.

A FINAL PRAYER

As the curtain to the Temple is torn in two, Jesus offers up these words, "Father, into your hands I commend my spirit" (Luke 23:46).

Some translations, such as the ESV and NIV, read, "Into your hands I commit my spirit." These are not just any words. Jesus is offering up a prayer. Jesus's entire life was fashioned and formed by prayer. There are more than twenty-two references to Jesus praying in the New Testament. He often went away to be alone with and pray to God. He prayed all night before choosing those who would be his disciples and later lead his church (Luke 6:12-13). He teaches his disciples to pray (Matthew 6:9-13; Luke 11:2-4). He prays in the Garden of Gethsemane before facing his own death (Luke 22:42-44; Matthew 26:42). The entire seventeenth chapter of the Gospel of John is dedicated to Jesus's prayer for his disciples and for us. In this beautiful and intimate prayer to his heavenly Father, Jesus asks that through him his disciples (and we) might come to know the one true God ("this is eternal life" [John 17:3]), be protected, have Jesus's joy completed in them, see his glory, and that his love that the Father has given him might be in them, and he might be in them. He prays that the Father, Son, and disciples might all be one.

It should be no surprise that Jesus's first words from the cross were in the form of a prayer for forgiveness for those who had betrayed, denied, abused, and killed him (Luke 23:34), or that he also cries out in prayer in his darkest moment, "My God, my God, why have you forsaken me?" (Mark 15:34). Finally, some of his last words from the cross were also a prayer; one that gave form to his life from a young age. It is a prayer that Mary would have taught him as a child. It is a prayer that Jewish boys and girls prayed before going to bed. It's much like the prayer many of us were taught as children:

> *Now I lay me down to sleep,*
> *I pray the Lord my soul to keep.*
> *If I should die before I wake,*
> *I pray the Lord my soul to take.*

If I should live for other days,
I pray the Lord to guide my ways.

As the words, "Father, into your hands I commend my spirit," are on Jesus's lips, the entirety of this prayer from Psalm 31, which Jesus certainly knows by heart, are no doubt on his mind as well. The psalm begins like this:

In you, O LORD, I seek refuge;
do not let me ever be put to shame;
in your righteousness deliver me.
Incline your ear to me;
rescue me speedily.
Be a rock of refuge for me,
a strong fortress to save me.

You are indeed my rock and my fortress;
for your name's sake lead me and guide me,
take me out of the net that is hidden for me,
for you are my refuge.
Into your hand I commit my spirit;
You have redeemed me, O LORD, faithful God.
                                    Psalm 31:1-5

The psalm continues:

Be gracious to me, O LORD, for I am in distress;
my eye wastes away from grief,
my soul and my body also.
For my life is spent with sorrow,
and my years with sighing;
my strength fails because of my misery,
and my bones waste away.

I am the scorn of all my adversaries,
a horror to my neighbors,

> *an object of dread to my acquaintances;*
> > *those who see me in the street flee from me.*
> *I have passed out of mind like one who is dead;*
> > *I have become like a broken vessel.*
> *For I hear the whispering of many—*
> > *terror all around!—*
> *as they scheme together against me,*
> > *as they plot to take my life.*
> > > Psalm 31:9-13

In quoting this psalm, Jesus surely must have remembered how the words of the other verses spoke to his situation: the plot to take his life, the failing of his strength, the horror on the faces of those who loved him and now watched him die. And yet, like so many of the psalms, when individuals and communities are at their lowest points and crying out to God, this psalm ends on a note of hope and even triumph:

> *Blessed be the LORD,*
> > *for he has wondrously shown his steadfast love to me*
> > *when I was beset as a city under siege.*
> *I had said in my alarm,*
> > *"I am driven far from your sight."*
> *But you heard my supplications*
> > *when I cried out to you for help....*
>
> *Be strong, and let your heart take courage,*
> > *all you who wait for the LORD.*
> > > Psalm 31:21-22, 24

Jesus has waited. God has heard. And so Jesus understands, when he commits his spirit into the Father's hands, that he is announcing not the end of a failed mission, not a victory by the earthly powers of violence and death, but a triumph by God that is expressed in the very next verse in the psalm: "You have redeemed me" (Psalm 31:5).

These last words that Jesus prays to his heavenly Father are words of hope, faith, and complete trust. This trust was developed through a lifetime of living in an intimate relationship with God. It came from years of living a life formed by the ingrained habits of prayer, worship, scripture reading, and loving and serving others. John Wesley called these habits "means of grace." Means of grace are not spiritual "chores" we can perform that earn points toward salvation. Rather, they are spiritual practices we engage in that provide a means of experiencing God's presence or grace—things that can bring us closer to God. Praying the scriptures was a means of grace that Jesus learned as a child and continued until his dying breath. It is revealing that two of his seven utterances from the cross are quotations from the Psalms that are offered as prayers. In his last words to us, Jesus once again gives us an example to pray in our own dark moments—a way to find his presence and comfort, and to trust him enough to place our lives and our spirit in his hands.

When Jesus says, "Into your hands I commend my spirit," he is using a word that is rich in theological meaning for the Jewish faith. In Hebrew, the word for *spirit* is *ruach*. The same word can also mean *breath* or *wind*. God breathed God's spirit, the breath of life, into the first human being (Genesis 2:7). Now, from the cross, Jesus completely entrusts his life, his spirit, into the Father's hands. Those hands are always ready to hold us in our times of uncertainty, fear, and darkness. They are hands that are standing ready to grasp our own if we will reach out to them. They are already reaching out to us.

A PARENT'S HANDS

As I think about Jesus's prayer, I've been thinking about the hands of my own father and mother. They were probably like the hands of your parents or grandparents. They were hands that lifted me into a lap when I needed comfort; held tight to mine to keep me out of danger as we crossed the street; tenderly hugged me, held me, and wiped away tears. They were teaching hands that held me afloat until I could swim on my own, that kept the bicycle steady while I was learning to ride. They were hands that sheltered our family from danger during a tornado. They were hands that could be completely trusted.

When there was danger, when I was scared, when we walked through large crowds and could easily have become separated, my father or my mother would have me give them my hand. Then I could keep going without fear. I knew that I would not lose them while my hand was in theirs. My trust in my father and mother was absolute. In this same way, God's hands are always there to take our hands. "Even though I walk through the darkest valley, /" the psalmist wrote, "I fear no evil; / for you are with me" (Psalm 23:4). Even while they were physically nailed to the cross, Jesus put his hands in the hands of his Father; he trusted God to walk with him the rest of the way.

During the COVID-19 crisis, some of my congregation said that, in the beginning, sheltering in place was rather novel, like a little stay-cation. While it offered more time with family and more time to read and think about what's important in life, the reality of the long-term soon began to sink in. Some of the observations I heard were: "Homeschooling my children is a *lot* harder than I thought it would be! Teachers really DO need a raise!"

Working from home with children is a real challenge for parents, especially single parents. Some had family members in the medical field serving on the front lines of the pandemic, and they worried about infecting their families. We were all concerned about their safety and well-being. Many students had to forgo great rites of passage during their senior year of high school or college. They worried about placements in colleges or internships. Others worried about jobs and finances. And inevitably, we lost congregants, friends, or loved ones to death.

Pandemic or no, don't the same fears haunt us? We fear for the health of those we love and for our own. We worry about the state of affairs in the world. We get caught in the grip of darkness and stress over so much that we cannot control. For all of that, Jesus offers us the words of a prayer that can provide peace and certainty during our times of uncertainty and upheaval, for we have a heavenly parent and a Savior in whose hands our lives can be trusted. We have a God who walks with us, holds us, wipes our tears, and offers us protection as we walk through our darkest valleys. The worst feeling is not final. God holds our hand.

During Lent this past year, I encouraged my congregation to pray these words each day. I asked them, "What if we prayed 'Into your hands I commit my spirit,' or 'Into your hands I commit my life' every morning and every evening during this Lent and beyond? How could that help and sustain you in the days or weeks to come?" How could it help us overcome our anxieties? How could it help us put our complete trust in God and re-orient our perspective on life? How can it help us be more like the lilies of the field and the birds of the air, free to live beautifully as God made us and liberated by God from worrying about the things we cannot control?

For me at least, when I begin and end my days in prayers of trust, my fears subside. Those fears are replaced with peace, hope, and confidence in the One whose hands hold those I love and whose everlasting arms hold me. Though I may not know exactly what will happen in the time ahead, I know in whose hands my times are held, and I know I can trust those hands. Jesus's last prayer from the cross offers us encouragement and an example of how we should pray in times of uncertainty and darkness. It offers us a way to form our own lives in the very same way his mother helped him form his.

His was a life formed in trust and confidence in God. I think what Jesus wanted us to hear from the cross was this: "Into your hands I commend my spirit" are not words to die by. They are words that teach us how to live. They are words to live by.

After speaking his final words, Jesus bows his head and gives up his spirit (John 19:30); the literal reading of the original Greek is that he *"hands over"* his spirit, his breath, his life, into the hands of the One in whom he has complete trust. Jesus has been "handed over" to Pilate, Herod, and the crowds, and they believe they in turn have handed him over to death. However, Jesus is actually the one with the upper hand. He willingly hands over his life that we might have abundant and eternal life even in the midst of crisis and darkness.

IT IS *FINISHED*

In John's Gospel, Jesus's very last words offer just as much hope and encouragement as Jesus's words in Luke. In order to place those last words in context, let's back up and review what has happened at the cross in John's Gospel. Immediately after Jesus speaks to his mother and the disciple whom he loved standing near the cross, scripture tells us:

> *After this, when Jesus knew that all was now* finished, *he said (in order to fulfill the scripture), "I am thirsty." A jar full of sour wine was standing there. So they put a sponge full of the wine on a branch of hyssop and held it to his mouth. When Jesus had received the wine, he said, "It is* finished." *Then he bowed his head and gave up his spirit.*
>
> John19:28-30, emphasis added

Jesus knows all is now finished. After Jesus drinks the sour wine offered to him from the hyssop branch, he expends his last ounce of energy and breath to say, "It is finished." What does Jesus mean by "it"? And what does he mean by "finished"?

While Jesus's human suffering is certainly coming to an end—finished—these words have, as is always the case in the Fourth Gospel, a deeper and more symbolic meaning that begs for ears to listen. This is not a cry of defeat in death, but of victory. In John's Gospel, Jesus is always presented as in control of everything that happens to him. He always knows what is happening and what is going to happen. He knows that the time will come for him to be arrested and crucified. He knows that Judas will betray him (in spite of that, he does not exclude Judas from his last meal with the disciples; think about *that* the next time you are invited to the communion table). He rebukes Peter for striking the high priest's servant because he knows that he must walk the path that leads to Golgotha.

Jesus's last words in John's Gospel are actually one word in Aramaic or Greek—*tetelestai*. It means "Finished!" or "Completed!" The word shows up several times in John's Gospel. When Jesus's disciples show surprise that he has been talking to an outsider, the Samaritan woman at the well, and sharing the news with her that he is the Messiah, he responds to them: "My food is to do the will of him who sent me and to *complete his work*" (John 4:34, emphasis added).

In the next chapter, Jesus says: "The works that the Father has given me to *complete*, the very works that I am doing, testify on my behalf that the Father has sent me" (5:36, emphasis added).

And on the night before he is crucified, Jesus prays:

> "And this is eternal life, that they may know you, the only true God, and Jesus Christ whom you have sent. I glorified you on earth by finishing the work *that you gave me to do*. So now, Father, glorify me in your own presence with the glory that I had in your presence before the world existed."
>
> *John 17:3-5, emphasis added*

On the cross, the work that the Word incarnate was sent to earth to perform was finished. Jesus is announcing: "Mission accomplished."

Often in John's Gospel, Jesus says, I have come to complete the work the Father has given me to do. It is Jesus, the Father's only Son, who makes God known to us (1:18) through his acts of mercy and love, as he uses his own hands to feed the hungry, to heal the sick, to wash his disciples' feet, to teach us by example what it means to love one another as he has loved us. In his dying words, Jesus is saying, My work on earth, for your behalf, is completed.

But is the work really, really finished? Or does his work bring a new beginning? *"Tetelestai,"* in the way Jesus uses this word on the cross, describes something that is completed but has ongoing, far-reaching implications for the future. You may recognize in *tetelestai* the root "tele," which we find in English words like telescope (to see far) and telephone (voice or sound from afar). Jesus's mission is complete. But the repercussions of his saving work extend for all time.

Jesus's work of rescuing us from sin and death is complete. He has overcome the worst in humanity that we might live like him. His work of offering forgiveness—complete. His work of showing us what the sacrificial love of God's looks like—complete. His actions on earth demonstrating the true character and love of God—complete. His creating a way for his church and his mission to continue—complete. His example of how our lives should be formed in his and like his to experience eternal life, now and beyond death—complete. His reconciliation of God and humanity, eliminating any distance, any veil between us—finished! Jesus left nothing undone or unsaid before he died. All that he wanted us to hear, learn, experience, and emulate was evident and completed on the cross. Jesus's work *on earth* is finished, but his work *in us* and in the world is ongoing.

His work to show God's love, care, and mercy to those who suffer, who are sick, who are hungry, who are isolated and alone, who are alone at home with children, who are fighting for all of our lives—that God's will be done on earth as it is in heaven—*that work* is ongoing in us and through us as God's daughters and sons. There is a work yet to be done.

The cross is not a defeat. It is God's defining revelation of love so pure, so complete, that it pours itself out for us in the knowledge that love wins the victory over human fear, human hate, and human violence. As Paul tried to explain it to the new Christians of Corinth, the idea of a crucified Messiah may seem like foolishness to people steeped in Greek culture; it may be a stumbling block to those among the Jews who expected the Messiah to be a ruler with military might; "but to us who are being saved it is the power of God" (1 Corinthians 1:18).

The question for us then becomes: What will we let God do in our hearts and in our lives?

As Paul professed, to be "in Christ," with Christ working within us, is to participate in Christ's work of reconciling, transforming love. And so he could write: "So if anyone is in Christ, there is a new creation: everything old has passed away; see, everything has become new! All this is from God, who reconciled us to himself through Christ, and has given us the ministry of reconciliation; that is, in Christ God was reconciling the world to himself, not counting their trespasses against them, and entrusting the message of reconciliation to us" (2 Corinthians 5:17-19).

When we "participate in Christ," when we follow the path marked out for us as disciples, we allow ourselves to become a canvas on which God paints a masterpiece of love—pouring ourselves out in acts of grace and mercy for others; trusting fully in God (and inspiring others to trust as well); offering forgiveness, even to those who wound us; offering others, through our examples, a glimpse of God's kingdom; living out what it means to be a new kind of family connected by God's love; thirsting for what is just and right; remaining faithful to our calling and our mission to the end.

We cannot always know how the witness we offer to Christ may change the lives of others we barely know and in ways we may never see. As we make our journey to the cross, we are called to sow cross-shaped seeds of love, justice, forgiveness, and reconciliation. We are called to water seeds others have planted in Christ's name and to tend to God's field. But it is God, as Paul reminded us, who gives the increase. And, following Jesus, it is in God we trust. It is God upon whom we cast our hope and our cares.

As we come to the end of this study, I pray that you hear with clarity how Jesus's last words were meant for you. During this Lenten season, as you draw closer to the cross, may you find a thin place where heaven and earth intersect and where you can experience the hands of the living God guiding your life, lifting you up, drying your tears. Most of all, may God bless your hands *and* feet as you answer the call to take up your cross and follow where Jesus has walked, sowing seeds of the Kingdom along the way. And may God grant you the faith to pour yourself out in love, for all of your life, until you are able one day to complete your mission and to say, as a faithful servant, "Into your hands, Lord, I hand over my spirit." Amen.

ACKNOWLEDGMENTS

It is my hope as a minister (as it is with most ministers) that the words I speak and write will lead others to experience the unfathomable magnitude of God's love, grace, and redemption through Jesus the Christ. And so, I am grateful to you, the readers who have intentionally joined me on this Lenten journey as we lean in and listen to the last and most important words Jesus speaks to each of us. I pray that those "Seven Words" have deepened your understanding of, and your relationship with, Christ, and that through God's grace they will be an inspiration to you in your journey toward Easter and beyond.

I am grateful to Susan Salley, and my editor, Maria Mayo, at Abingdon Press, for inviting me to write this book. I will be forever indebted to you for your confidence in placing this study in my hands, and for your encouragement and guidance in bringing *Seven Words* to life. Maria's meticulous editorial skills and insight were instrumental in ensuring that the words on the page reflected the intention that you, the reader, would experience the holy privilege of intimacy with the One who died wanting you to know how deeply you are loved. If any mistakes are among these pages, they are mine. Innumerable others on the Abingdon team were also invaluable in producing this book. To Alan Vermilye for making sure *Seven Words* found its way into your hands, and to Tim Cobb, Randy Horick, and all the team at Abingdon who have made this book a reality, please accept my heartfelt "thank you." You are the best!

To Trenton Waterson and his production team at Collaborate Media, thank you for making the long drive to Dallas when COVID-19 prevented us all from flying to Nashville to film the DVD! Your work in filming and editing was masterful. What a joy it was to work with you.

To Gail Hansard, Ann Williams, Carol Harris, Cheryl Vandiver, Vicki Smith, and Kay Porter, thank you for *always* asking about the book and for your constant encouragement and prayers.

I am blessed to be pastor to the Cox Chapel community at Highland Park United Methodist Church. Thanks to all of you for listening to the beginnings of this book in sermon form during Lent 2020. The sharing of your own stories, book recommendations, and follow-up theological conversations helped give shape to this book in more ways than you can know.

Finally, I want to thank my husband, Ike. Without your constant love, support, and understanding, this book would not be possible. Thank you for your endless patience and sacrificial love. I am so grateful to God for you and the life we share.

NOTES

Introduction

1 "Must Jesus Bear the Cross Alone" (Thomas Shepherd, 1855), from *The United Methodist Hymnal* (Nashville: The United Methodist Publishing House, 1989), 424.

2 "Lift High the Cross" (George William Kitchin and Michael Robert Newbolt, 1916), from *The United Methodist Hymnal*, 159.

Chapter 1: Father, Forgive Them

1 "Amazing Grace" (John Newton, 1779), from *The United Methodist Hymnal*, 378.

2 *Love Story*, directed by Arthur Hiller (1970; Los Angeles, CA: Paramount Pictures), Paramount Movies, https://www.paramountmovies.com/movies /love-story.

3 John Wesley, "I Felt My Heart Strangely Warmed" (May 24, 1738), in Chapter 2, *The Journal of John Wesley*, ed. Percy Livingstone Parker (Chicago: Moody Press, 1951), Christian Classics Ethereal Library, https://ccel.org/ccel/wesley /journal/journal.vi.ii.xvi.html.

4 Raymond E. Brown, *The Death of the Messiah: From Gethsemane to the Grave: A Commentary on the Passion Narratives in the Four Gospels, Vol. 2*, ed. David Noel Freedman (New Haven and London: Yale University Press, 1994), 975–980.

5 The story can be found at Corrie ten Boom, "Guidepost Classics: Corrie ten Boom on Forgiveness; In This Story from November 1972, the Author of *The Hiding Place* Recalls Forgiving a Guard at the Concentration Camp Where Her Sister Died," Guideposts, posted July 24, 2014, https://www.guideposts .org/better-living/positive-living/guideposts-classics-corrie-ten-boom-on -forgiveness.

6 Maria Mayo, *The Limits of Forgiveness: Case Studies in the Distortion of a Biblical Ideal* (Minneapolis, MN: Fortress Press, 2015), 186.

7 Mayo, *The Limits of Forgiveness*, 186.

Chapter 2: Today You Will Be with Me in Paradise

1 Brown, *The Death of the Messiah*, 1004.

2 Brown, *The Death of the Messiah*, 1012.

3   Eberhard Busch, "Proper 29 (Reign of Christ): Luke 23:33-43 (Theological Perspective)," in *Feasting on the Word: Preaching the Revised Common Lectionary, Year C, Vol. 4*, ed. David L. Bartlett and Barbara Brown Taylor (Louisville: Westminster John Knox Press, 2010), 336.

4   John Wesley, "The Scripture Way of Salvation: Sermon 43—1765," *John Wesley's Sermons: An Anthology*, ed. Albert C. Outler and Richard P. Heitzenrater (Nashville: Abingdon Press, 1991), 372.

5   Wesley, "The Scripture Way of Salvation," *John Wesley's Sermons*, 372.

6   *Dead Man Walking*, directed by Tim Robbins (1995; London: PolyGram Filmed Entertainment); "Matthew's Confession Scene," Fandango Movieclips, April 20, 2017, https://www.youtube.com/watch?v=6wyRTKGY2Tw&list=PLZbXA4lyCtqriqfqjdwyv9fEZzs-uIR88&index=6.

Chapter 3: My God, My God

1   Jenni Frazer, "Wiesel: Yes, We Really Did Put God on Trial," The Jewish Chronicle, September 19, 2008, https://www.thejc.com/news/uk/wiesel-yes-we-really-did-put-god-on-trial-1.5056.

2   Brown, *The Death of the Messiah*, 1046.

Chapter 4: Woman, Here Is Your Son

1   Robert F. Kennedy, "Day of Affirmation Address at Cape Town University" (speech), June 6, 1966, Jameson Hall, Cape Town, South Africa, transcript, American Rhetoric, page updated December 22, 2019, https://www.americanrhetoric.com/speeches/rfkcapetown.htm.

2   Gail R. O'Day, "John," in *Women's Bible Commentary: Expanded Edition with Apocrypha*, ed. Carol A. Newsom and Sharon H. Ringe, second edition (Louisville: Westminster John Knox Press, 1998), 383.

3   "Teilhard's Quotes: Quotes Attributed to Teilhard," American Teilhard Association, http://www.teilharddechardin.org/index.php/teilhards-quotes.

4   Victoria Emily Jones, "The Unnamed Emmaus Disciple: Mary, Wife of Cleopas?," Art and Theology, April 28, 2017, updated March 19, 2020, https://artandtheology.org/2017/04/28/the-unnamed-emmaus-disciple-mary-wife-of-cleopas/.

Chapter 5: I Am Thirsty

1   Brown, *The Death of the Messiah*, 1065.

2   Brown, *The Death of the Messiah*, 1077.

3   See "The Prayer of Saint Francis" (Francis of Assisi, Italy, 13th cent.), from *The United Methodist Hymnal*, 481.

Chapter 6: Into Your Hands

1   Marek Zabriskie, "The Thin Place of Iona," *The Living Church*, November 6, 2014, https://livingchurch.org/2014/11/06/thin-place-iona/.

Made in the USA
Coppell, TX
15 February 2023

12883661R00072